Birds of Guyana

Clifmond Shameerudeen

Table of Contents

About the author

Born and raised in Guyana, I was fascinated as a boy by the migratory birds that frequented my seaside home. This book is one of the ways I advocate for the preservation of bird habitats by promoting the natural beauty of birds in their natural environments. Special thanks goes to Dr. Floyd Hayes for mentoring me in my study of birds while I was a student at the University of the Southern Caribbean.

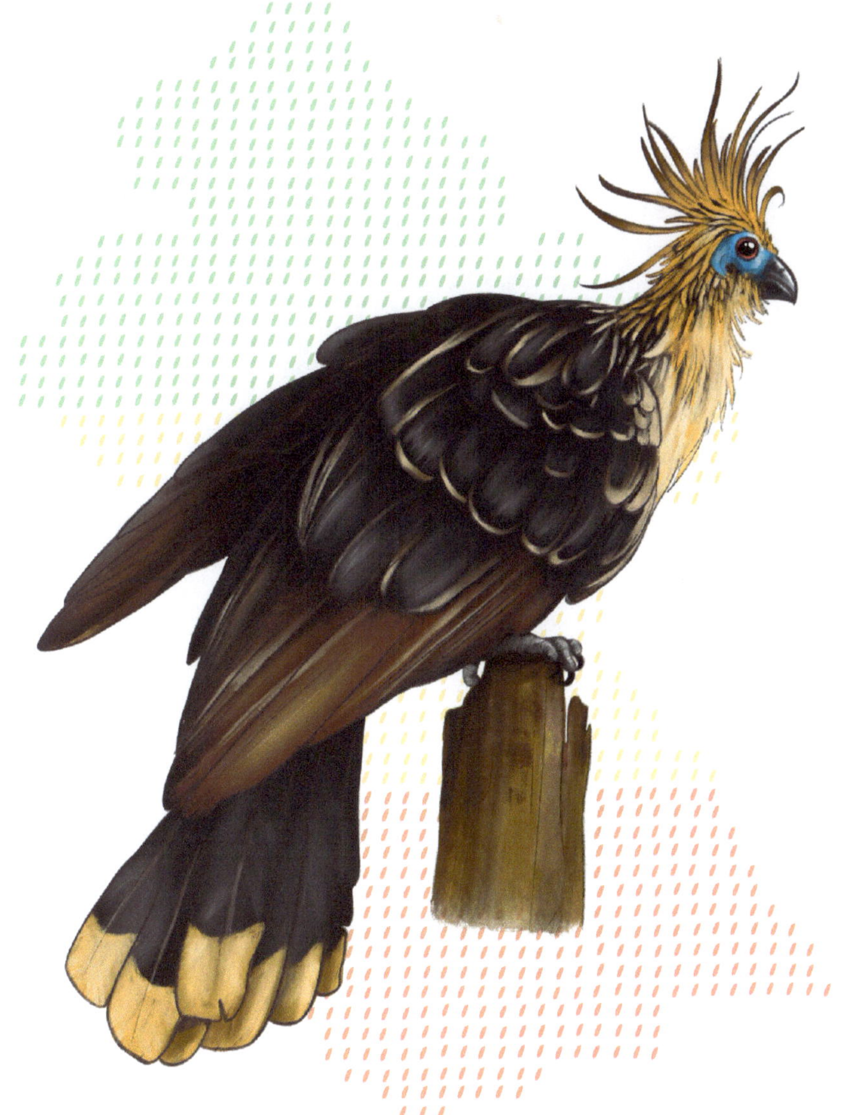

Hoatzin

Guyana's national bird is the Hoatzin, which is known locally as the Canje Pheasant. It lives along river banks and eats leaves. Because of its unique digestive system, which ferments the leaves it eats, the Hoatzin has an unpleasant manure-like odour.

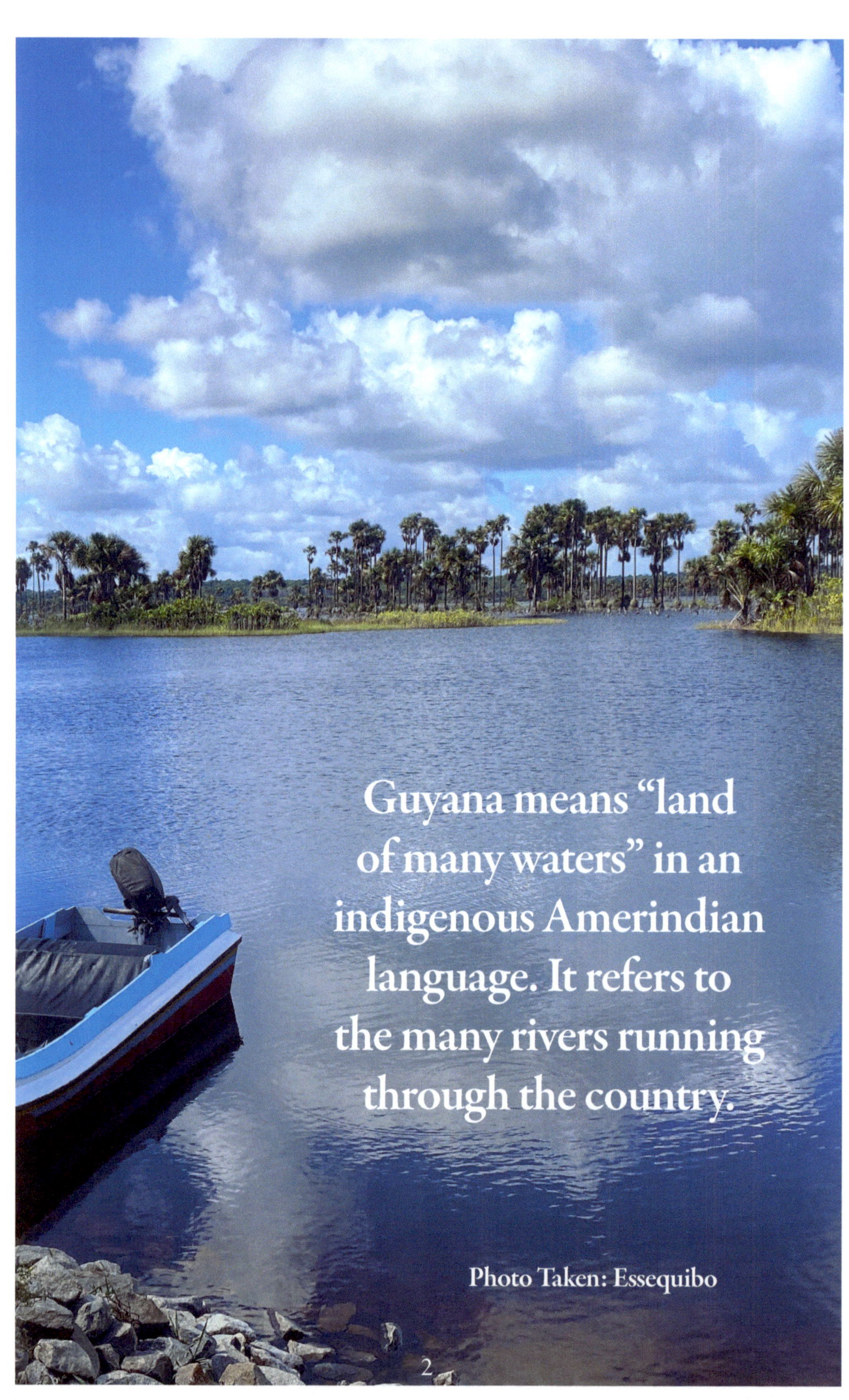

Guyana means "land of many waters" in an indigenous Amerindian language. It refers to the many rivers running through the country.

Photo Taken: Essequibo

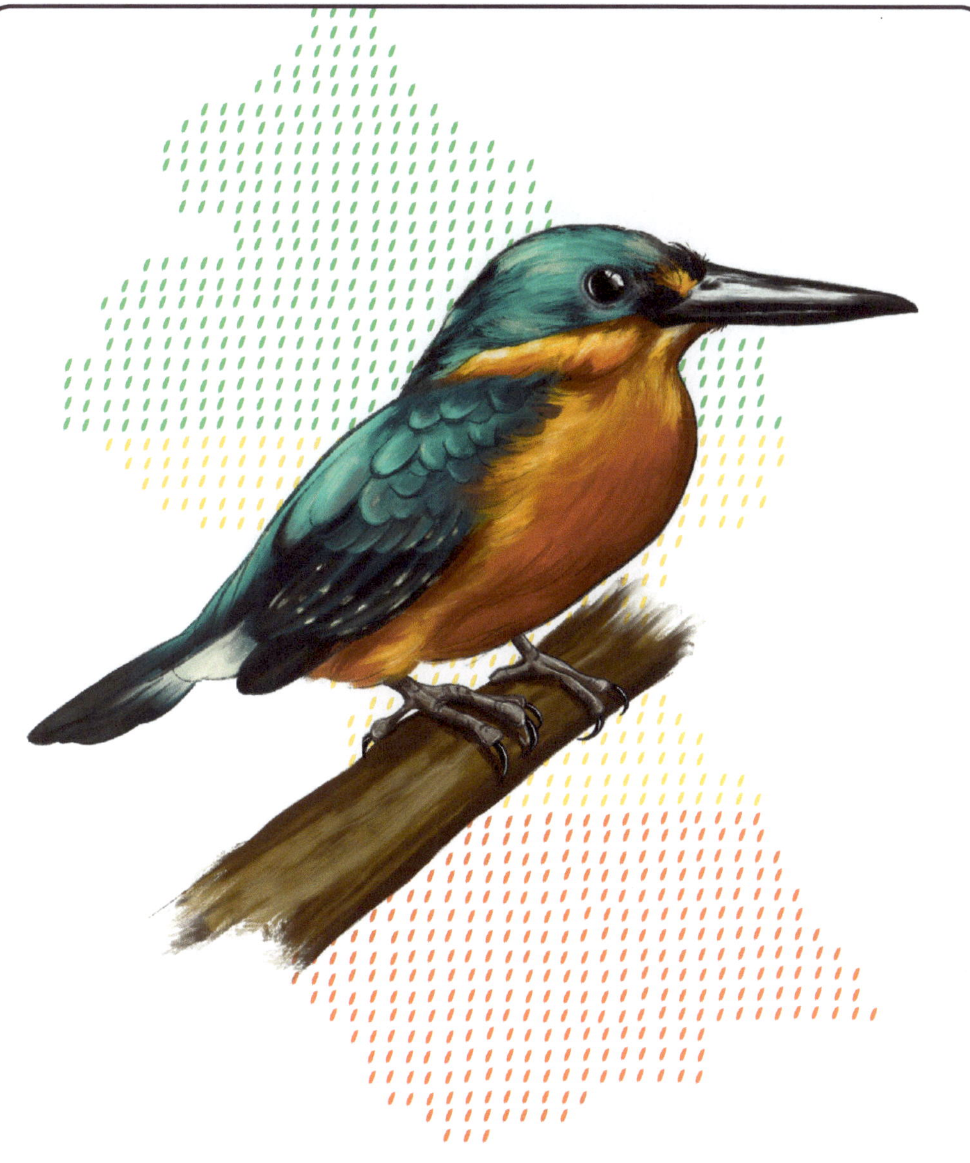

American Pygmy Kingfisher

Found throughout Guyana, this kingfisher is known for diving deep into the water to catch fish.

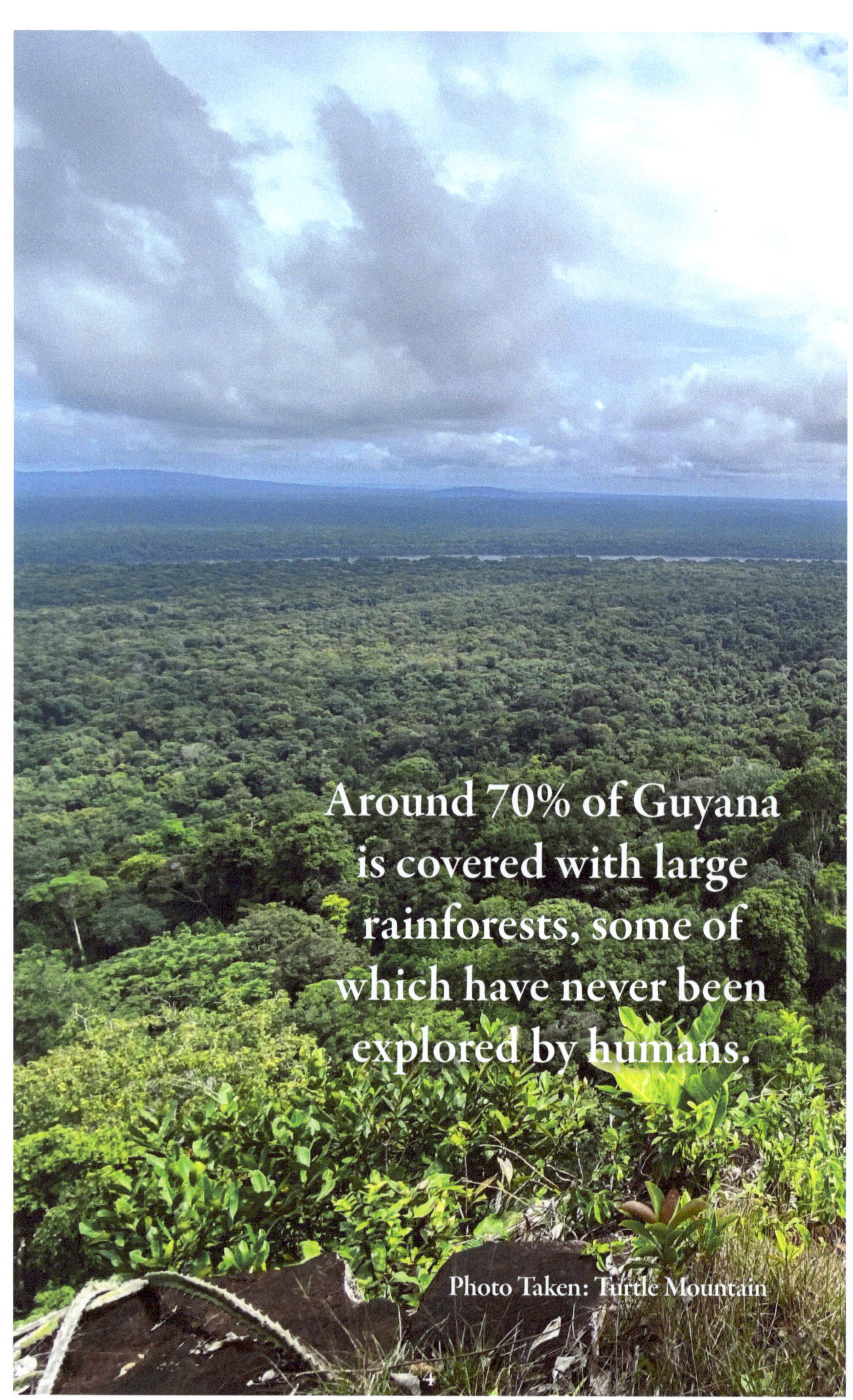
Around 70% of Guyana is covered with large rainforests, some of which have never been explored by humans.

Photo Taken: Turtle Mountain

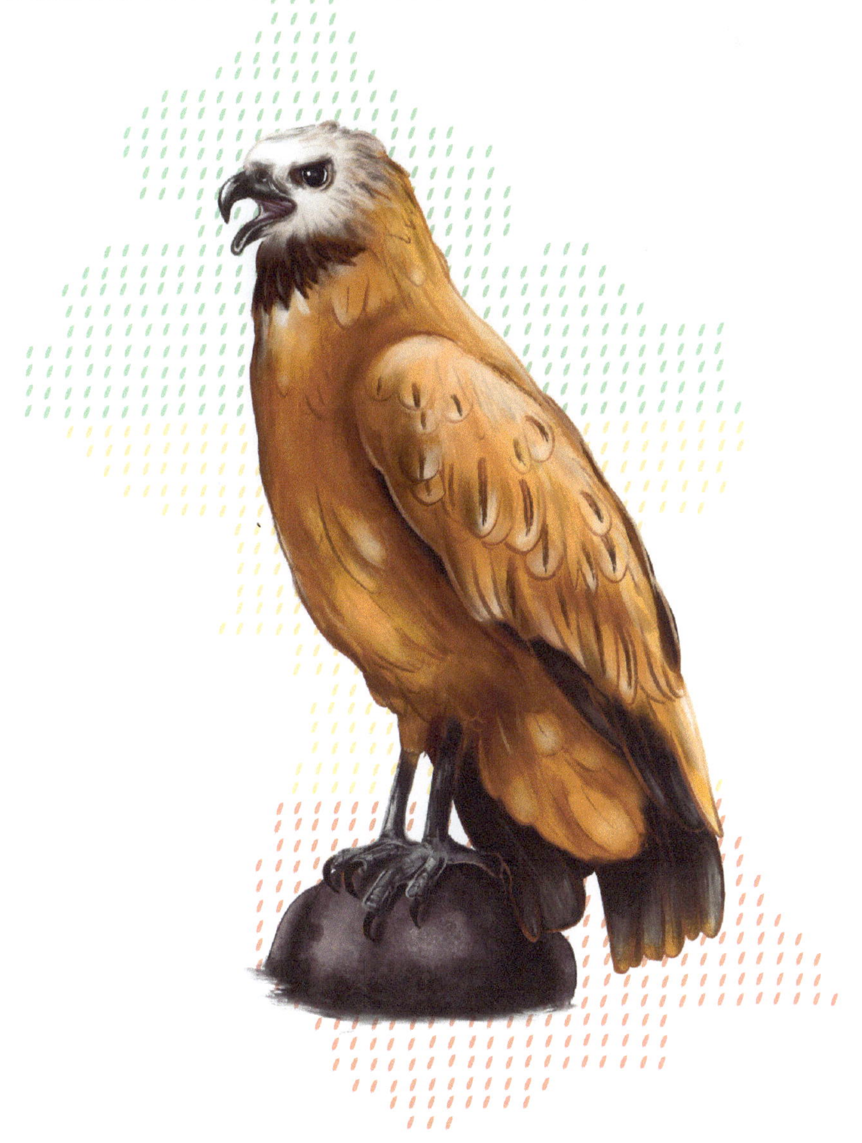

Black-collared Hawk

Found in Guyana's coastal areas, this raptor perches on low branches just above shallow bodies of water for easy access to the fish.

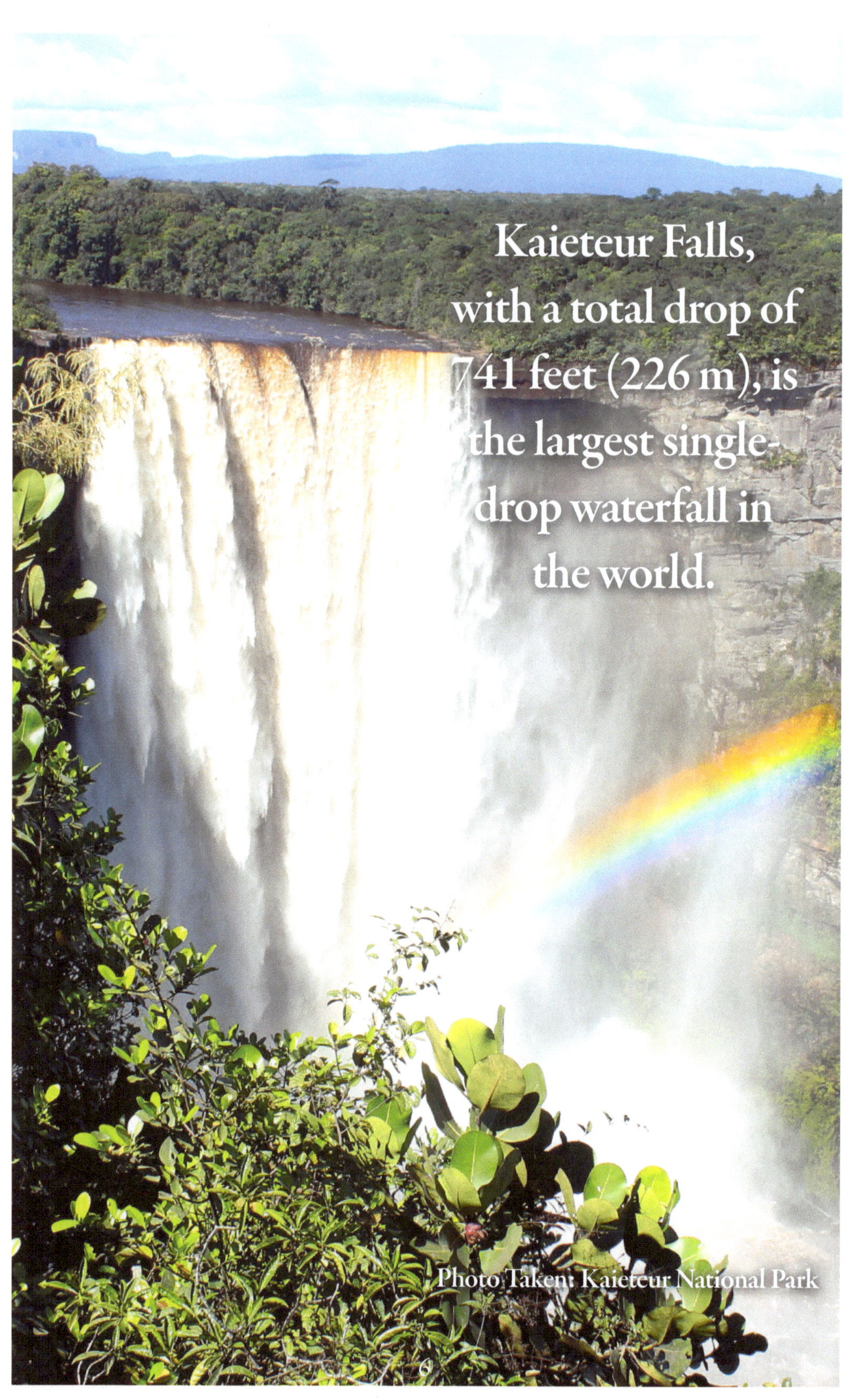

Kaieteur Falls, with a total drop of 741 feet (226 m), is the largest single-drop waterfall in the world.
Photo Taken: Kaieteur National Park

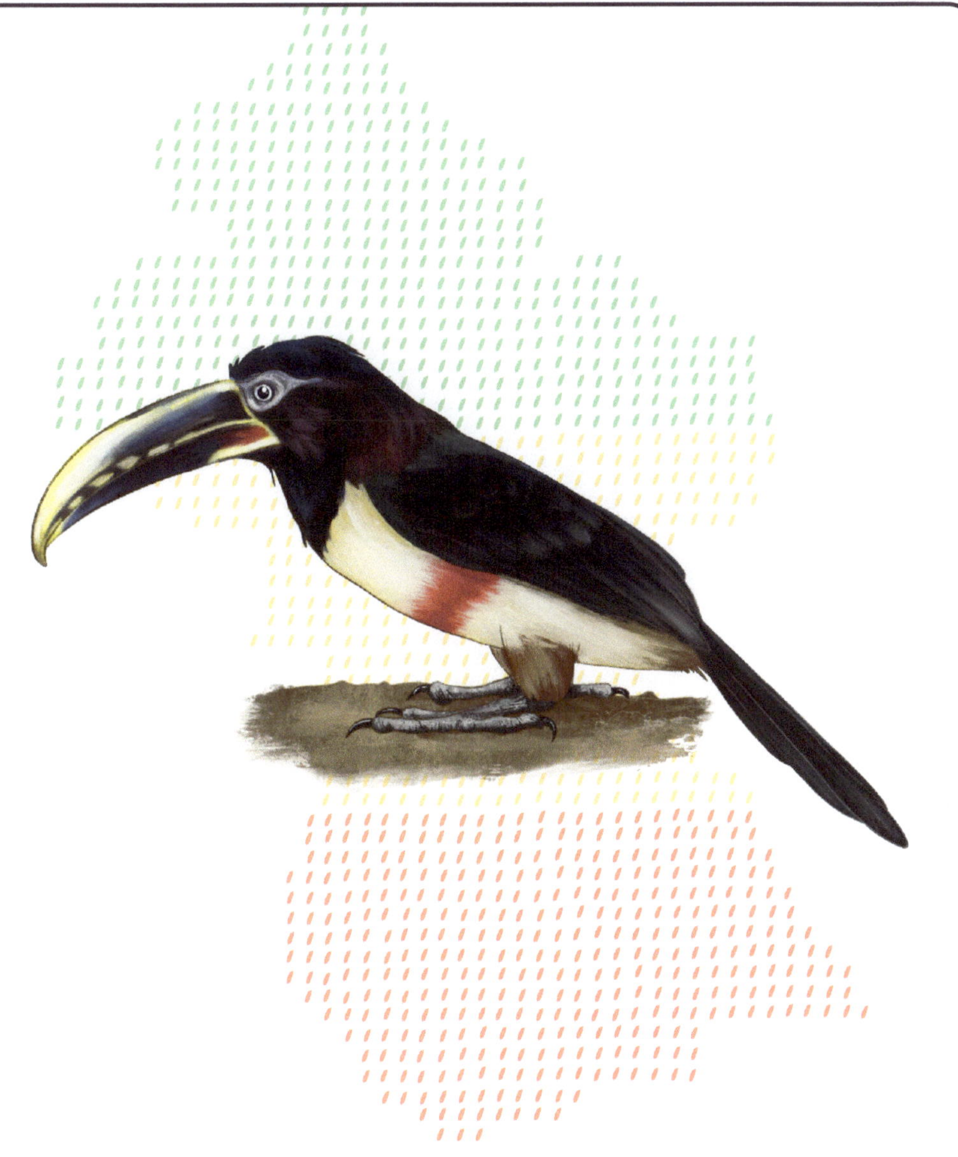

Black-necked Aracari

Found in lowland forests and sandy areas of Guyana, they feed on fruits and vegetables. They build their nests in abandoned woodpecker holes.

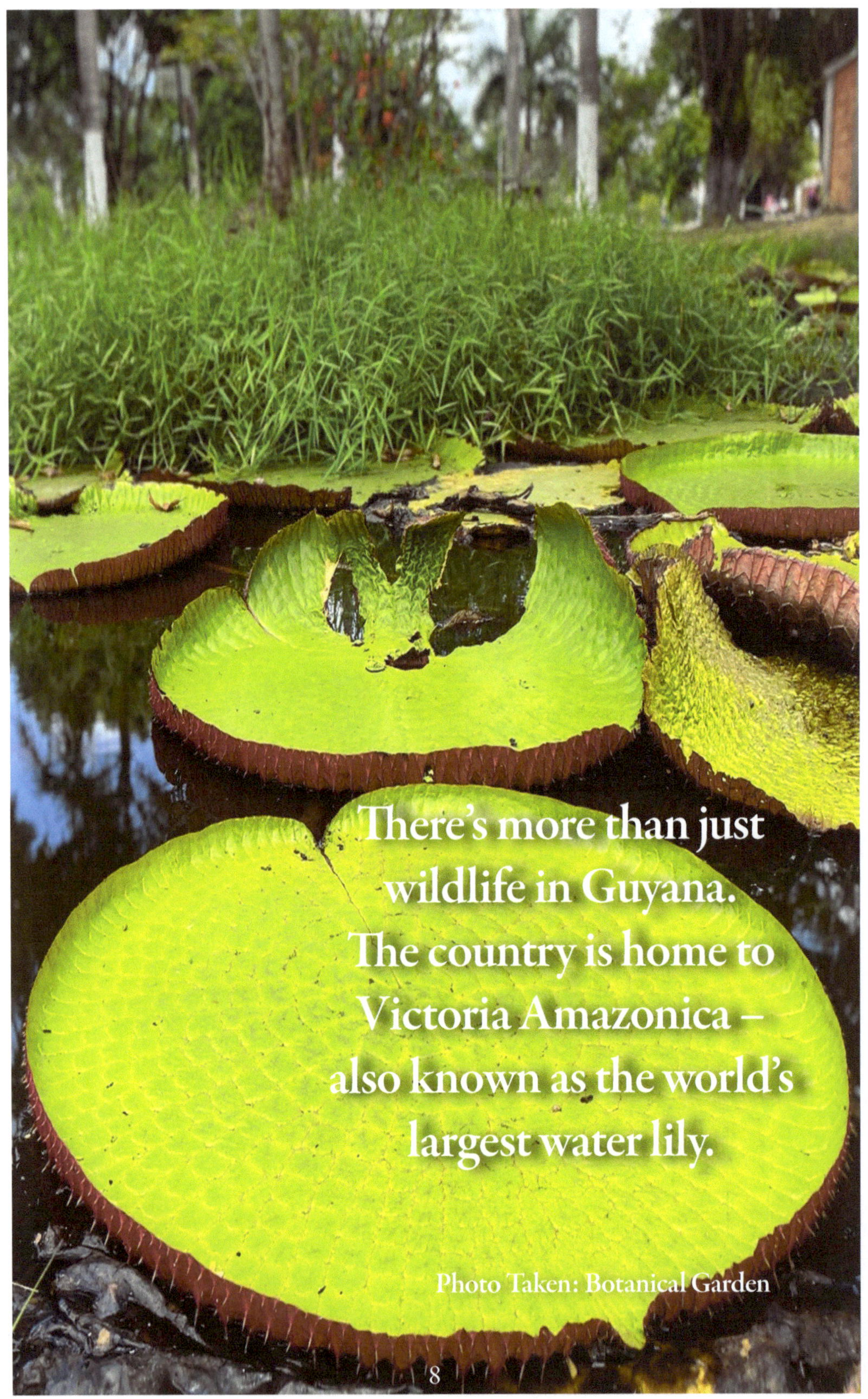
There's more than just wildlife in Guyana. The country is home to Victoria Amazonica – also known as the world's largest water lily.

Photo Taken: Botanical Garden

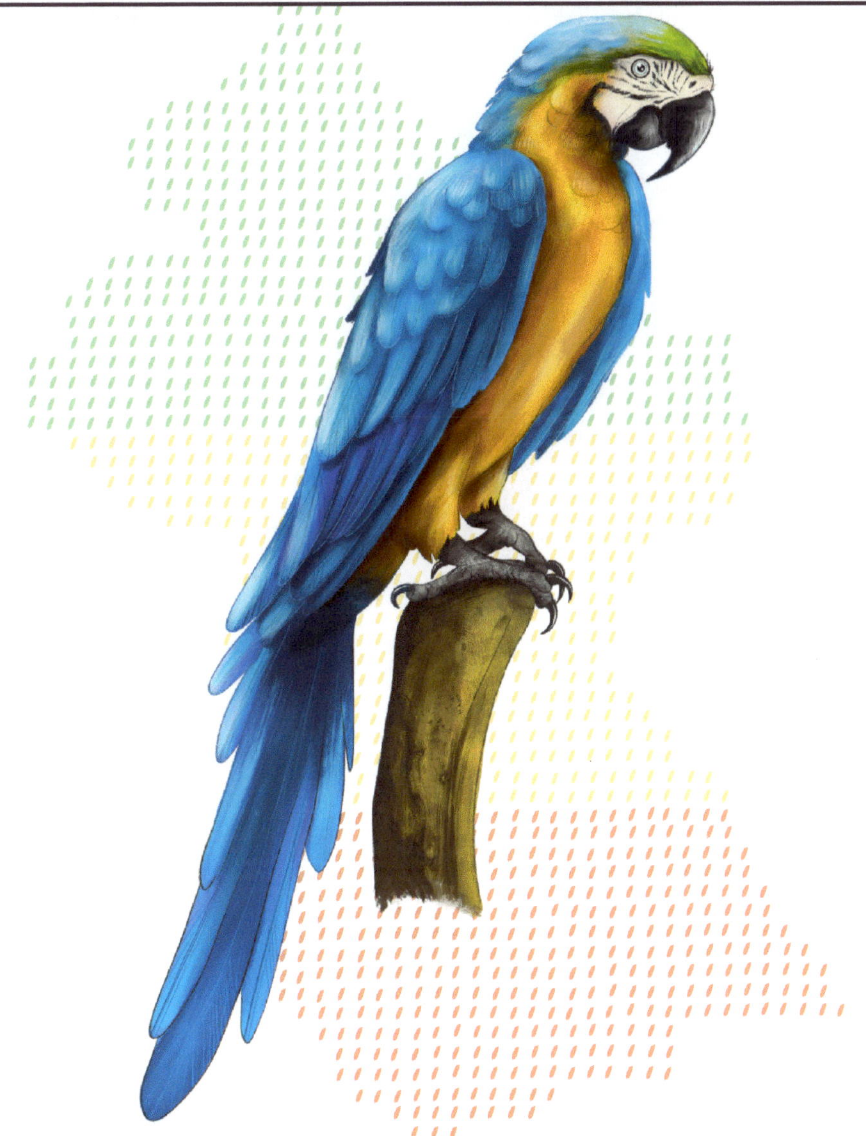

Blue and Yellow Macaw

This majestic bird can be seen in Guyana's botanical garden and above the canopy of Guyana's pristine rainforest. They mate for life and generally fly in flocks.

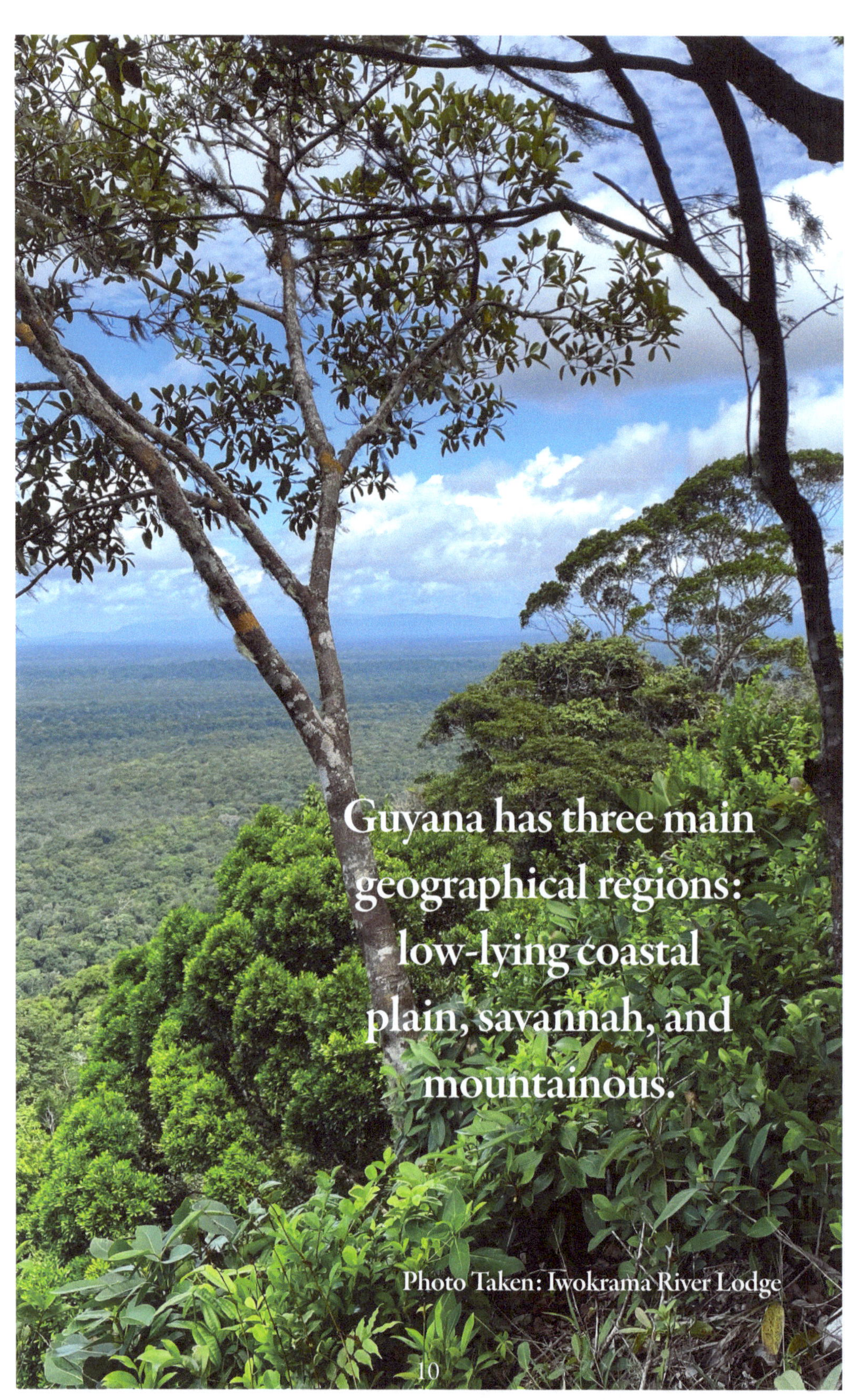
Guyana has three main geographical regions: low-lying coastal plain, savannah, and mountainous.

Photo Taken: Iwokrama River Lodge

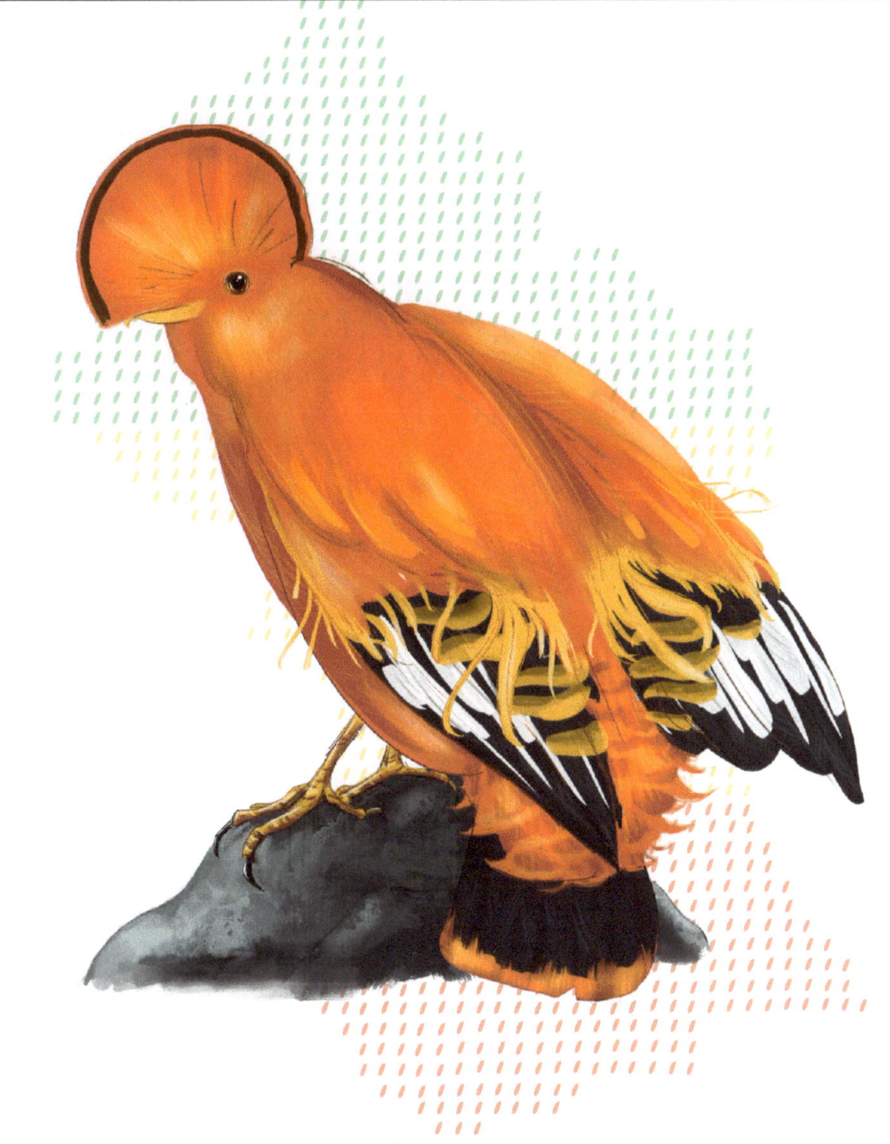

Guianan Cock-of-the-Rock

Found in the rainforests of Guyana, they build
their nests on rocks and ledges.

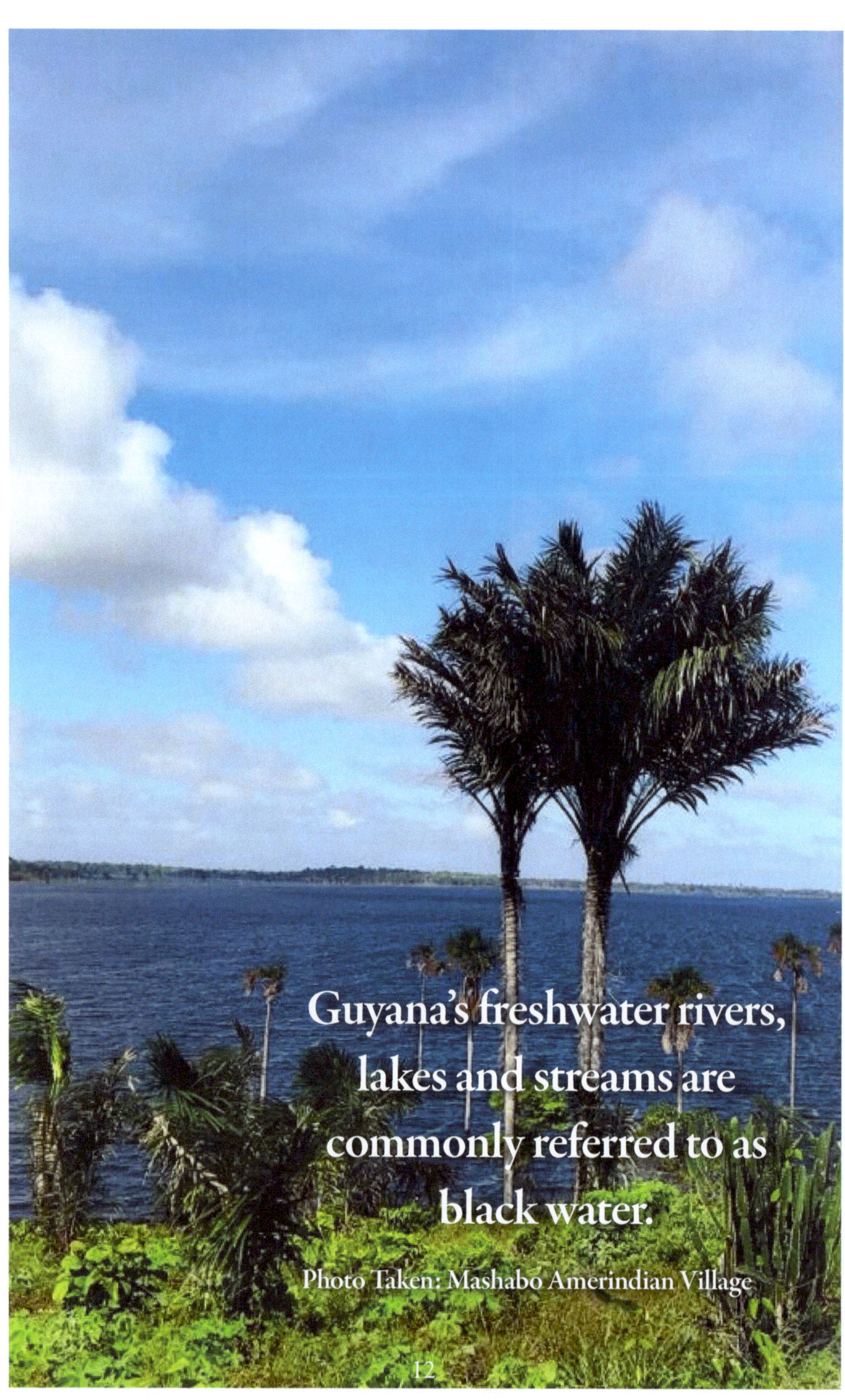

Guyana's freshwater rivers, lakes and streams are commonly referred to as black water.
Photo Taken: Mashabo Amerindian Village

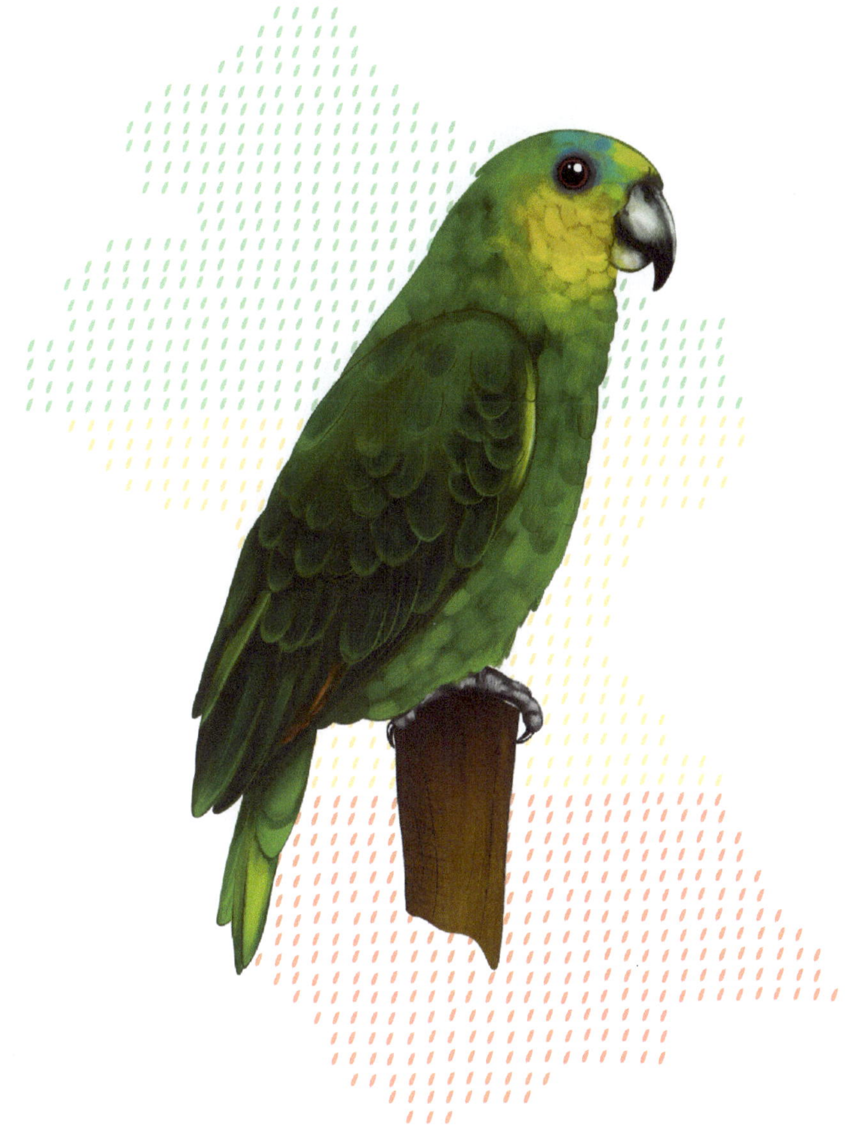

Orange-winged Parrot

Found in coastal areas, especially in Georgetown, this parrot sings loudly at sunrise and sunset. It is very distinct as it flies from palm tree to palm tree in search of food.

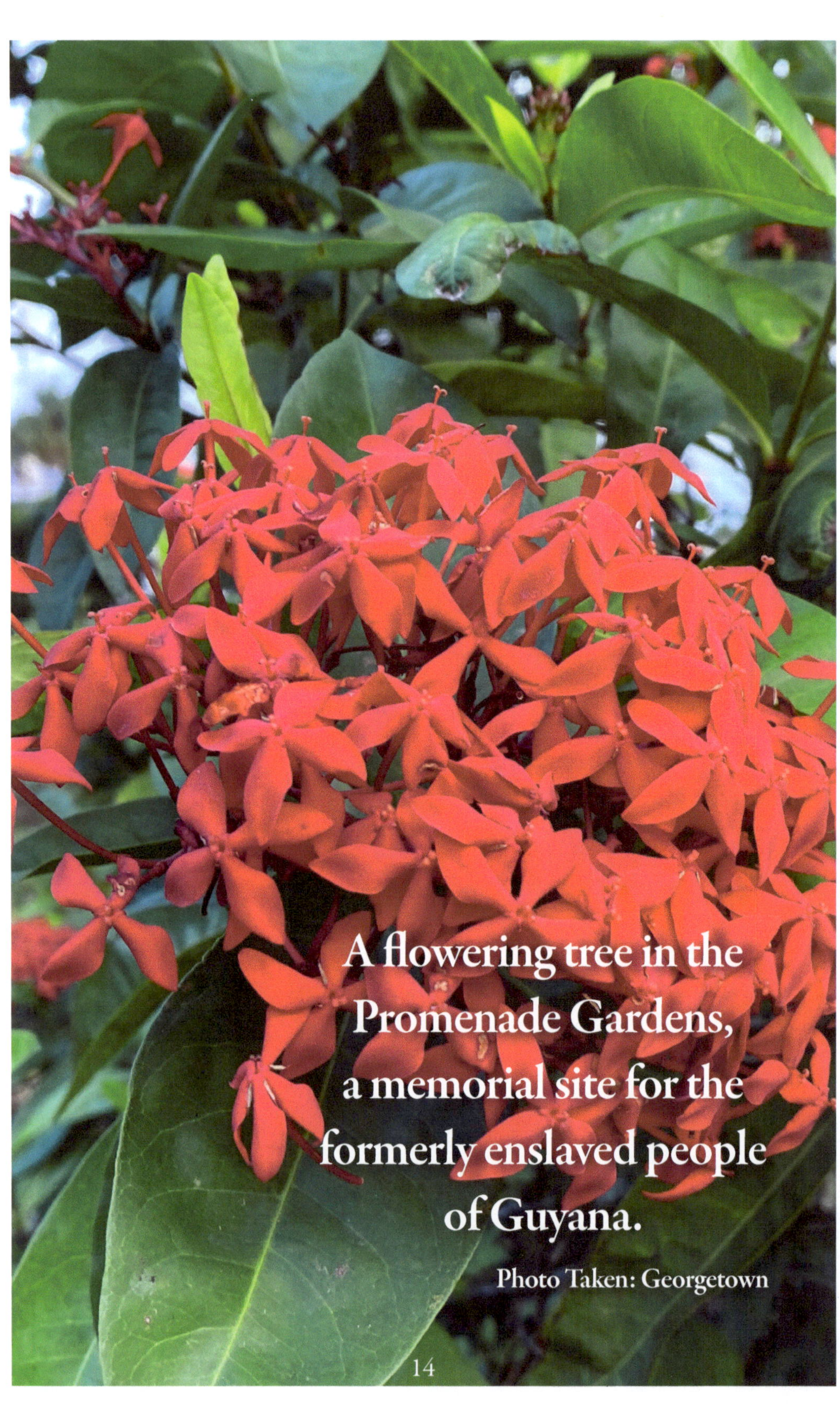

A flowering tree in the
Promenade Gardens,
a memorial site for the
formerly enslaved people
of Guyana.

Photo Taken: Georgetown

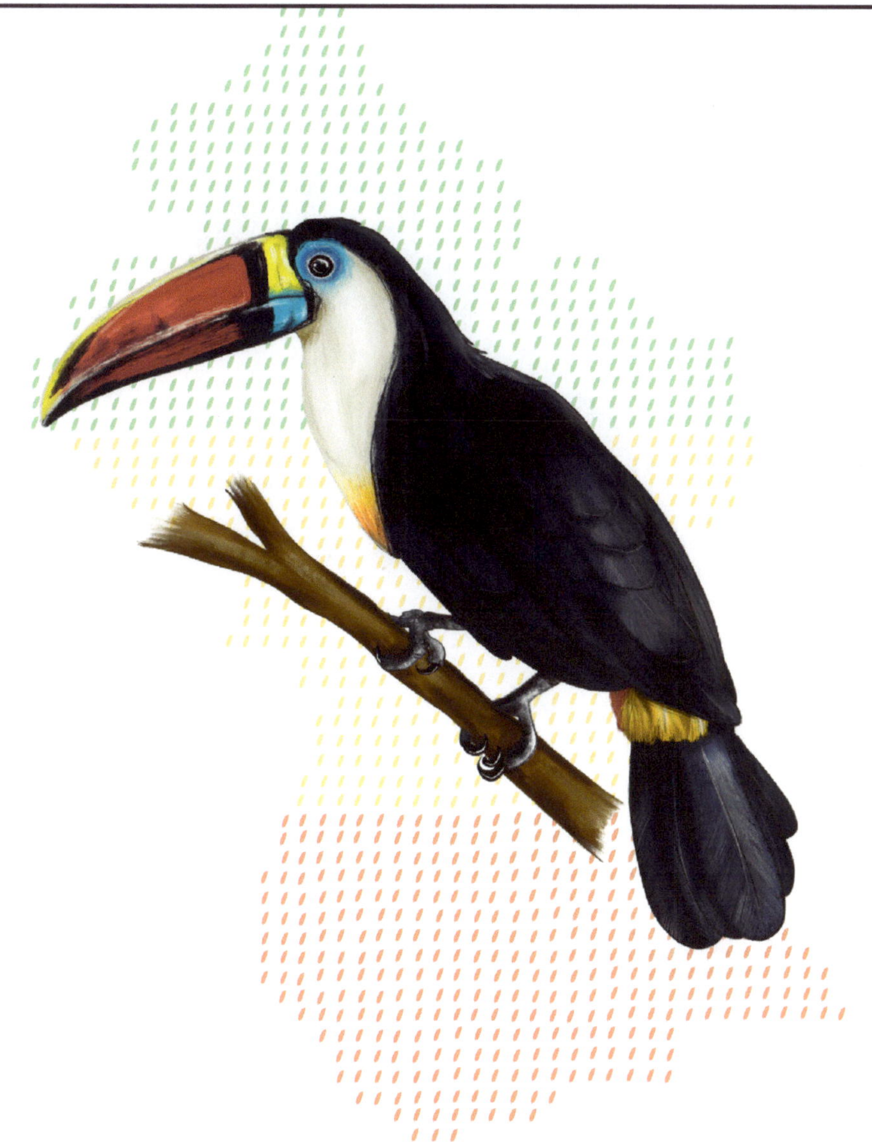

White Throated Toucan

Their loud, high-pitched calls can be heard over long distances in the lowland forests.

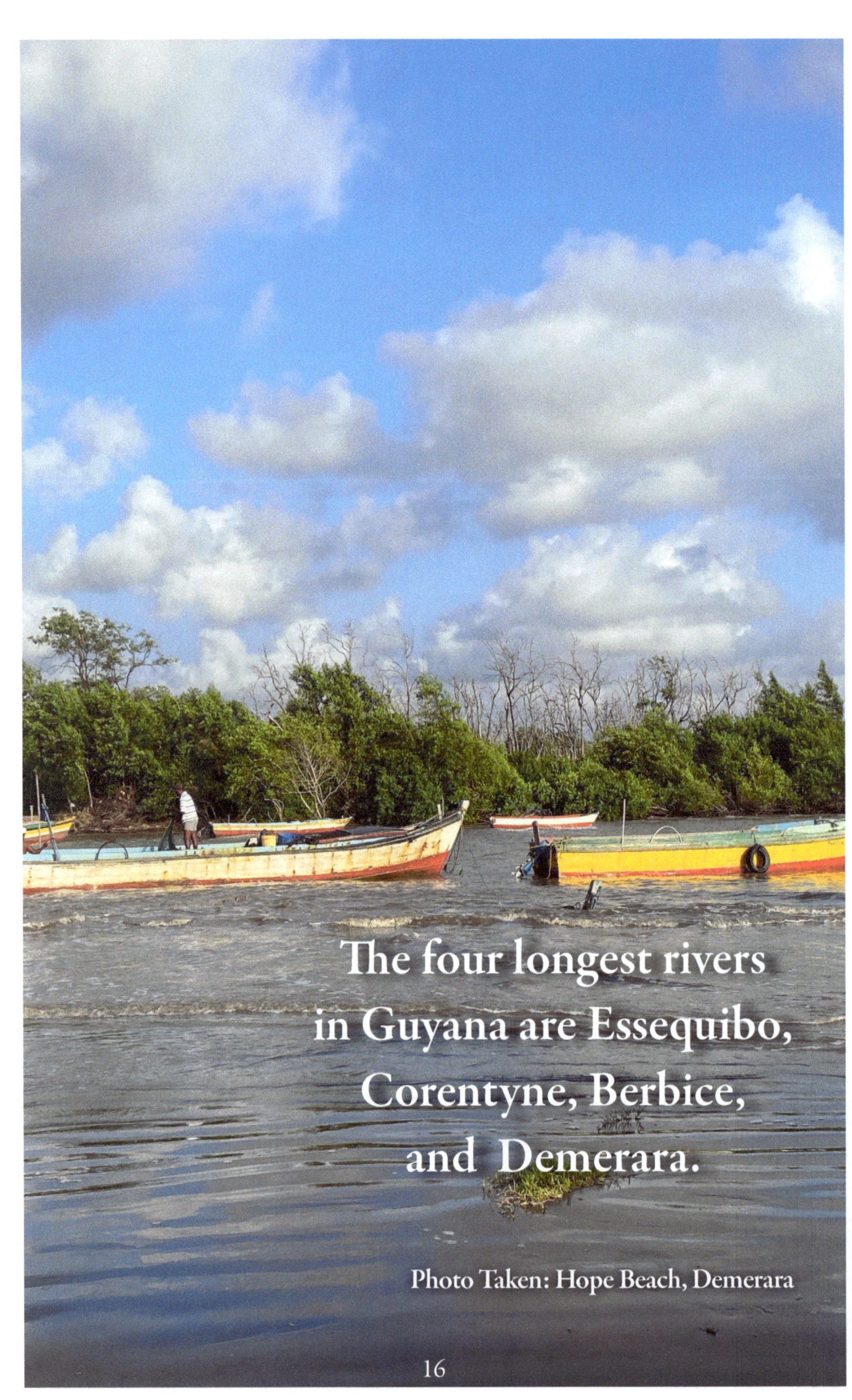

The four longest rivers
in Guyana are Essequibo,
Corentyne, Berbice,
and Demerara.

Photo Taken: Hope Beach, Demerara

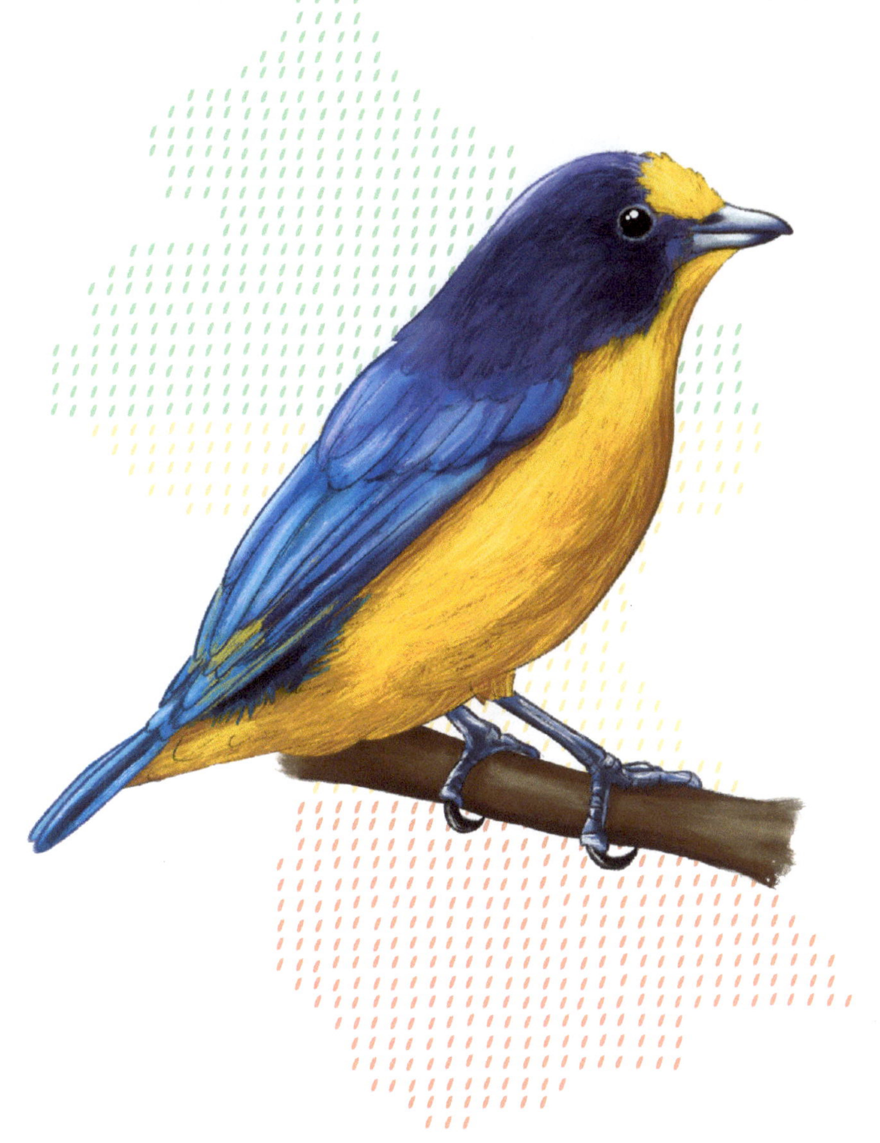

Violaceous Euphonia

You may find this colourful, pageant-ready bird, known for its singing, in Guyana's botanical garden.

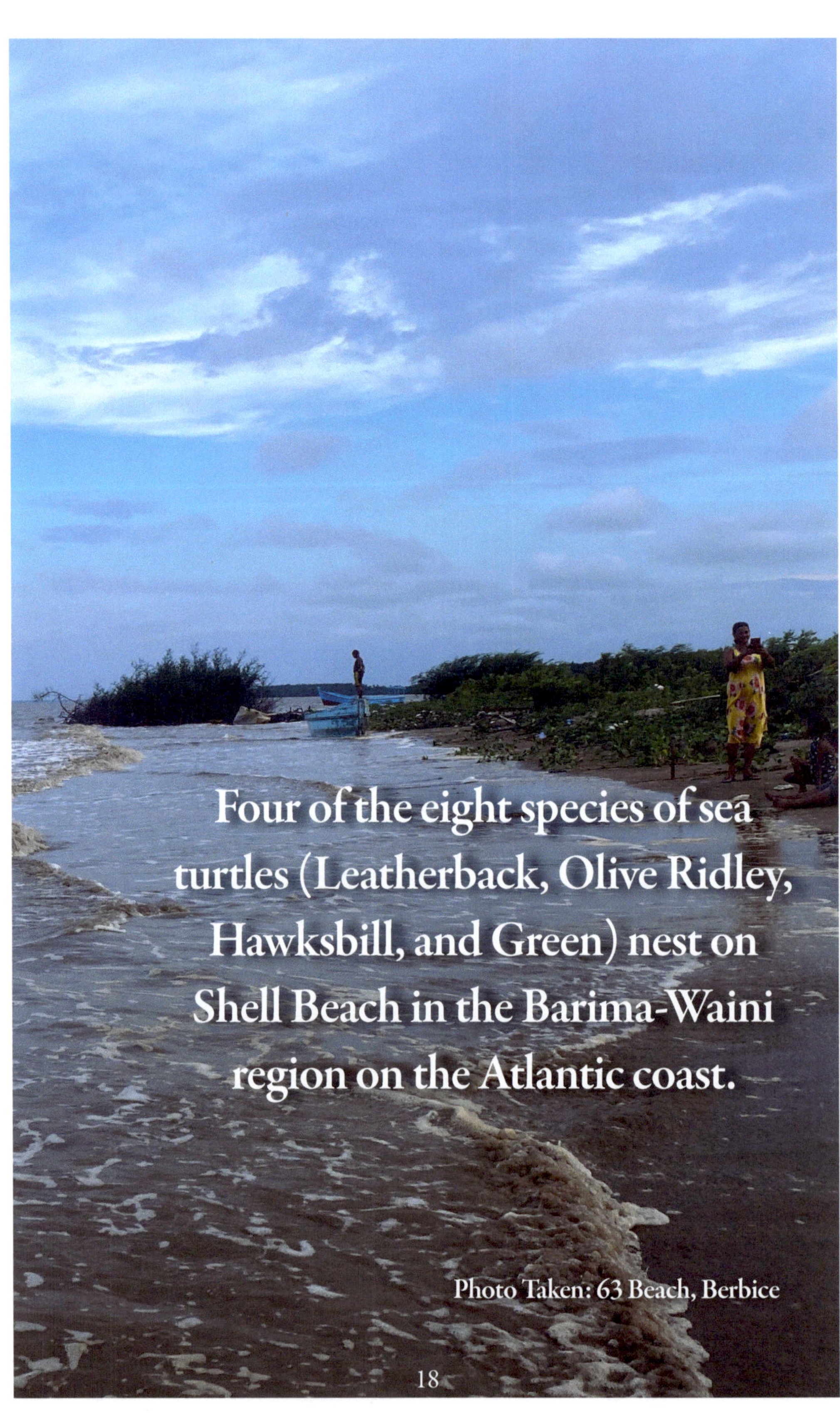

Four of the eight species of sea turtles (Leatherback, Olive Ridley, Hawksbill, and Green) nest on Shell Beach in the Barima-Waini region on the Atlantic coast.

Photo Taken: 63 Beach, Berbice

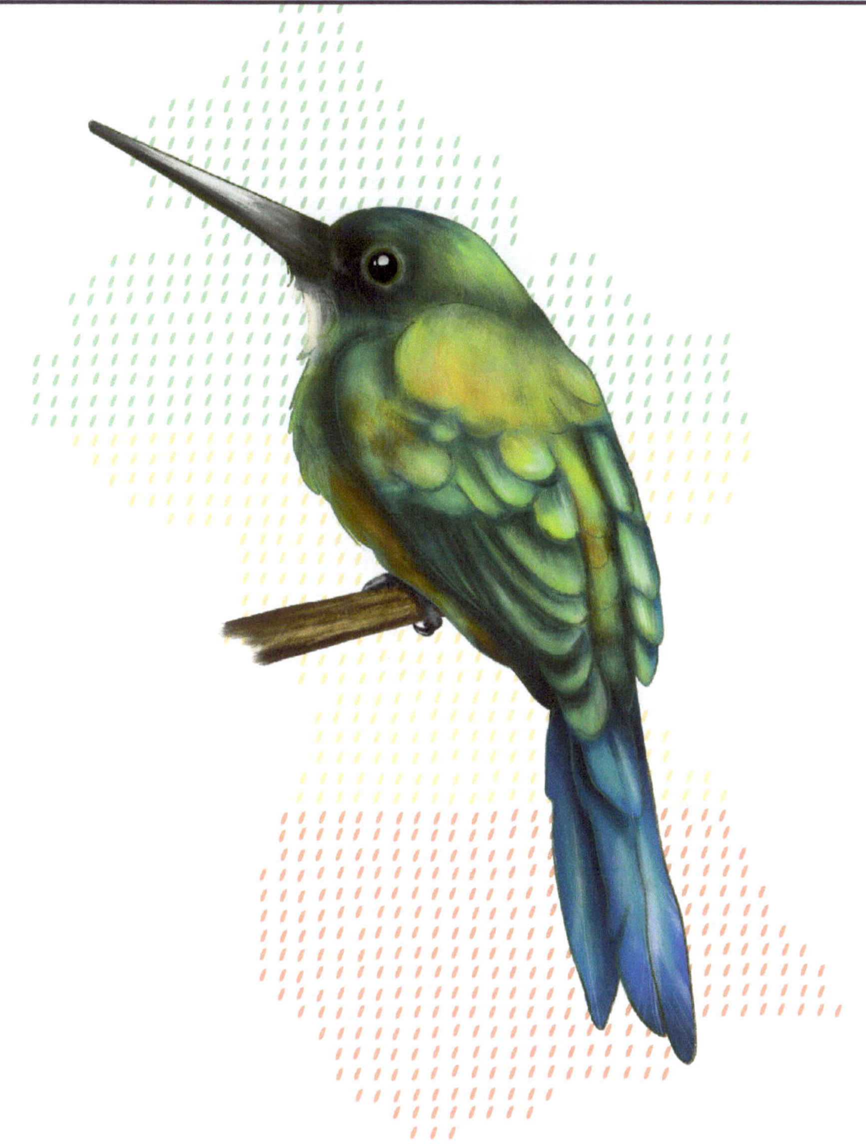

Green Tailed Jacamar

Living only in the Guiana Shield, it can be found in lowland river areas.

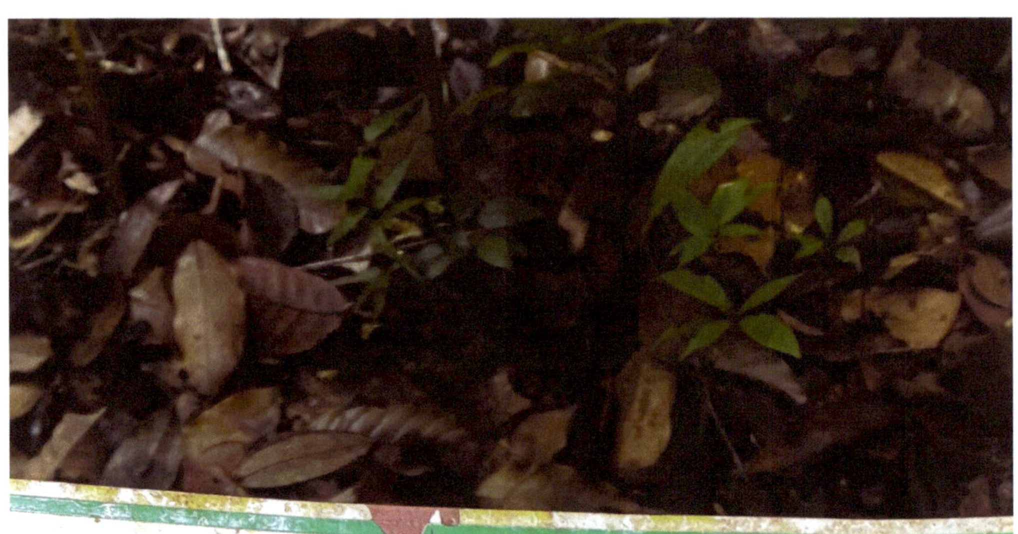

Greenheart
(Chlorocardium rodiei)

This extremely dense tree is found only in Guyana and is used worldwide for bridges walkways, wharves and docks due to its durability in contact with sea water. Locally it is used in the construction of houses.

Greenheart is an evergreen tree growing 15 to 30 meters tall with a girth of 35-60 cm.

Photo Taken: Iwokrama Rainforest

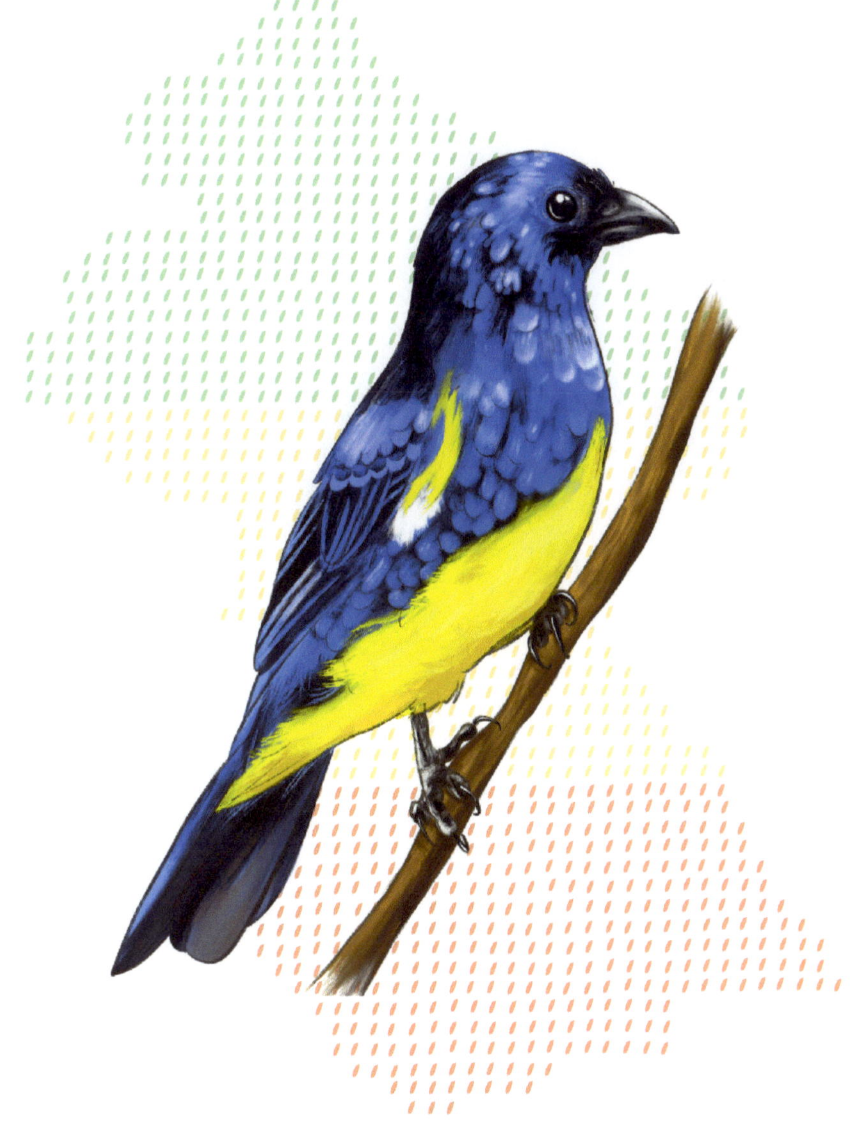

Tourquoise Tanager

This colourful bird can be found in Guyana's lowland areas. It is very sociable and prefers to fly in small flocks.

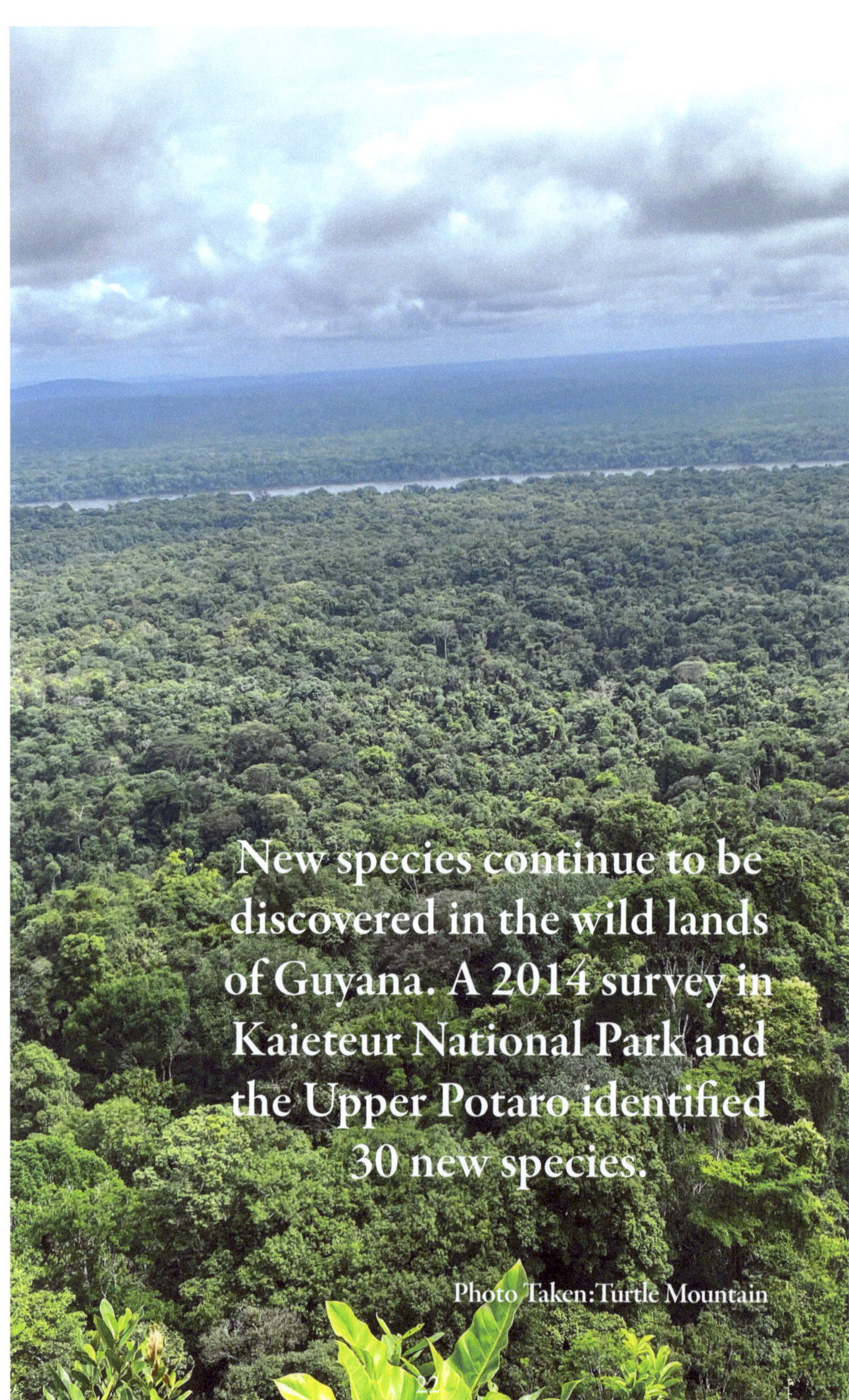
New species continue to be discovered in the wild lands of Guyana. A 2014 survey in Kaieteur National Park and the Upper Potaro identified 30 new species.

Photo Taken: Turtle Mountain

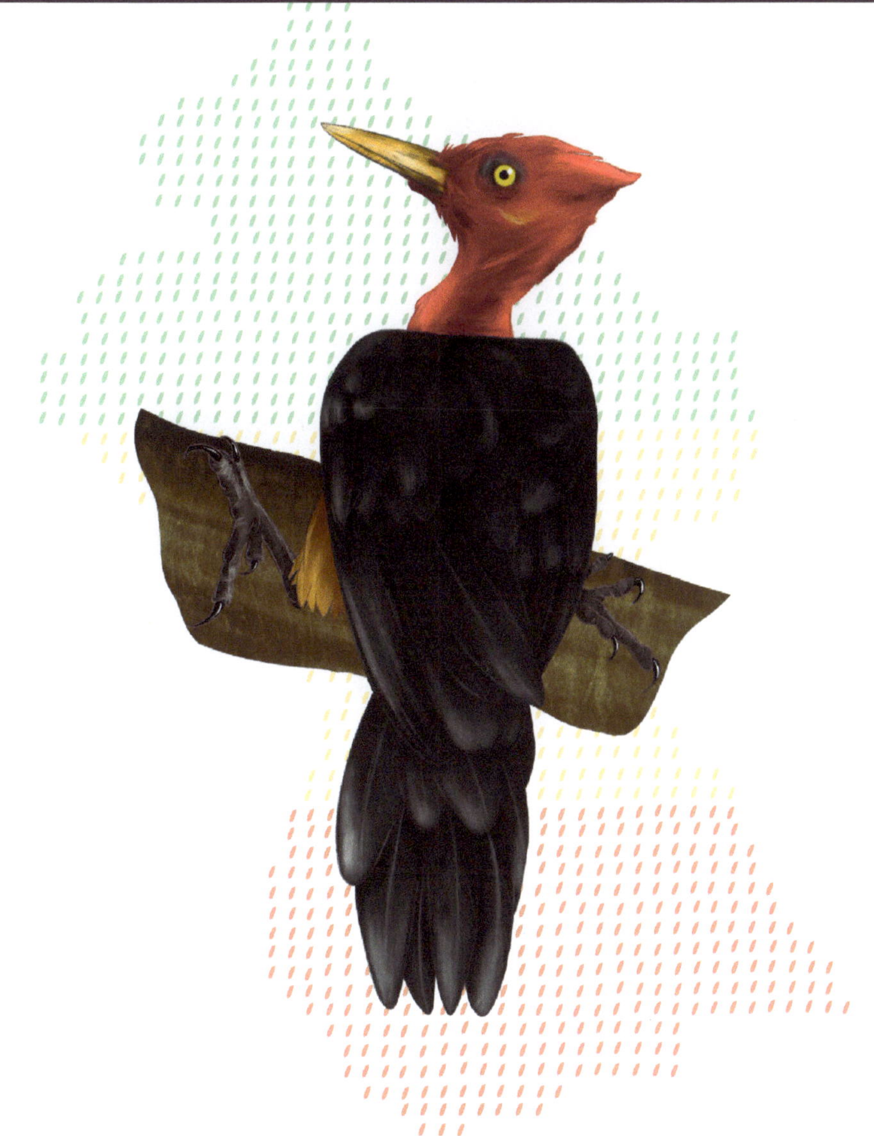

Red-necked Woodpecker

Found in Guyana's rainforests, both male and female have a redneck.

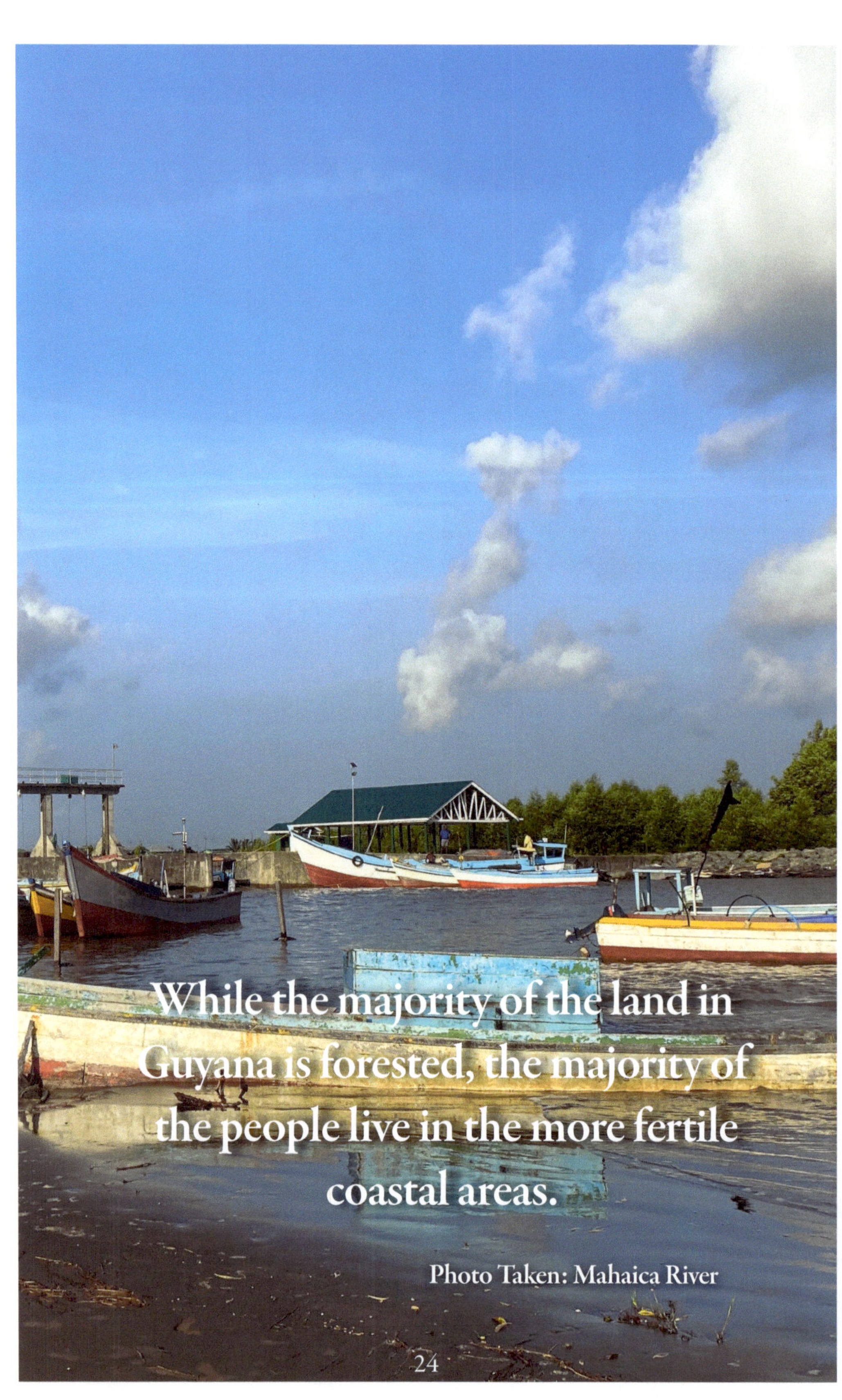
While the majority of the land in Guyana is forested, the majority of the people live in the more fertile coastal areas.

Photo Taken: Mahaica River

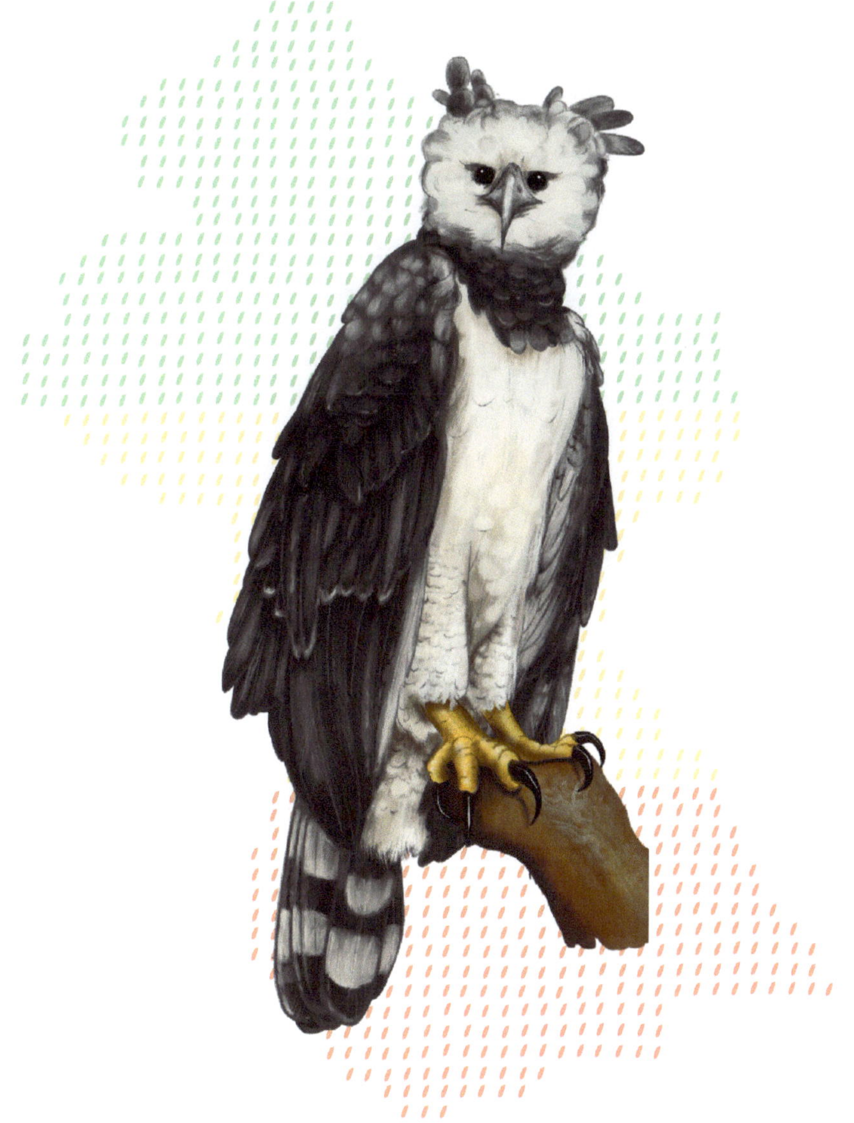

Harpy Eagle

This is the most powerful eagle in the world with a wingspan of 6.5 feet (2 meters). It can pursue its prey at 50 mph (80 kmh). With some patience, it can be spotted in Guyana's rainforests.

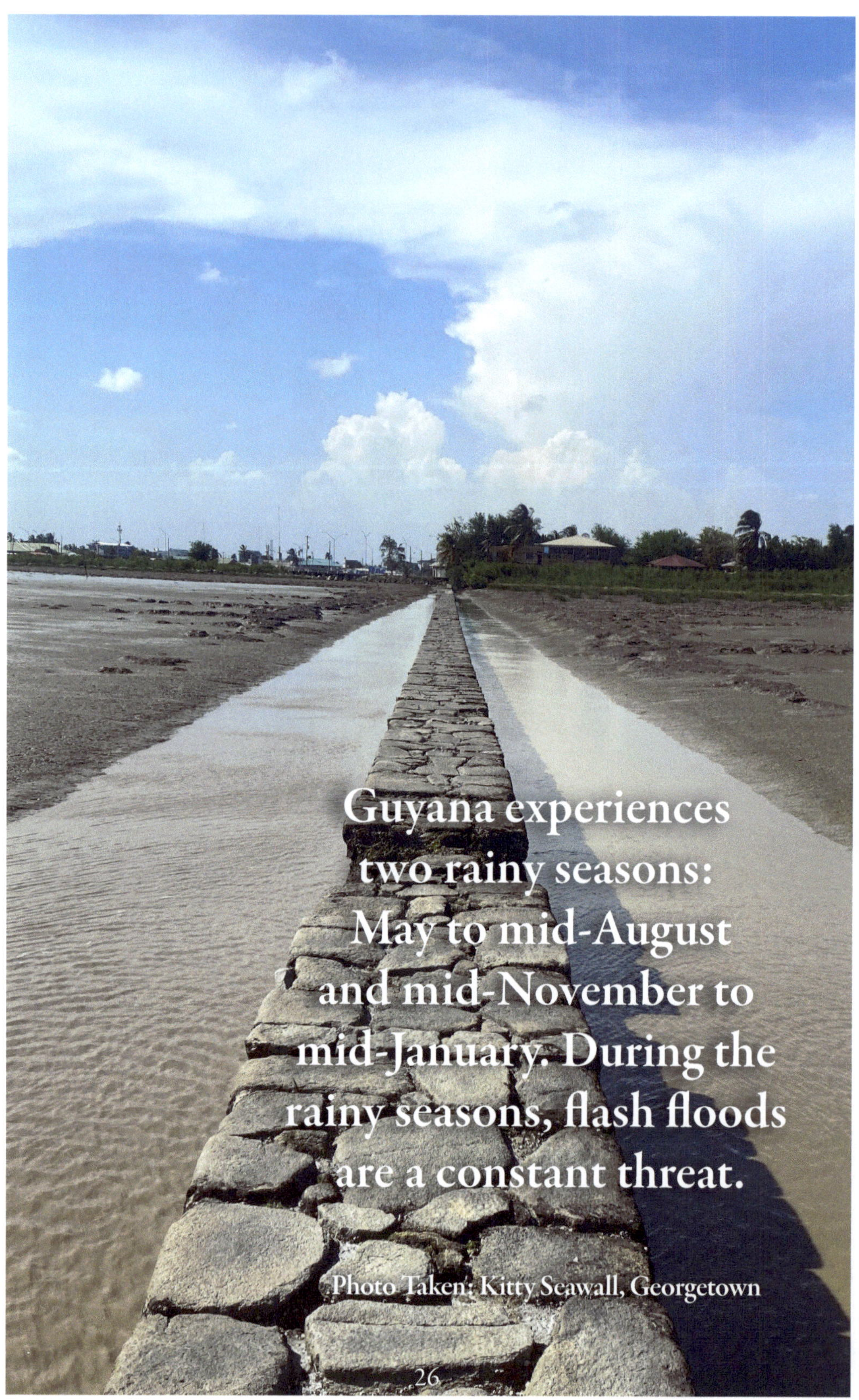

Photo Taken: Kitty Seawall, Georgetown

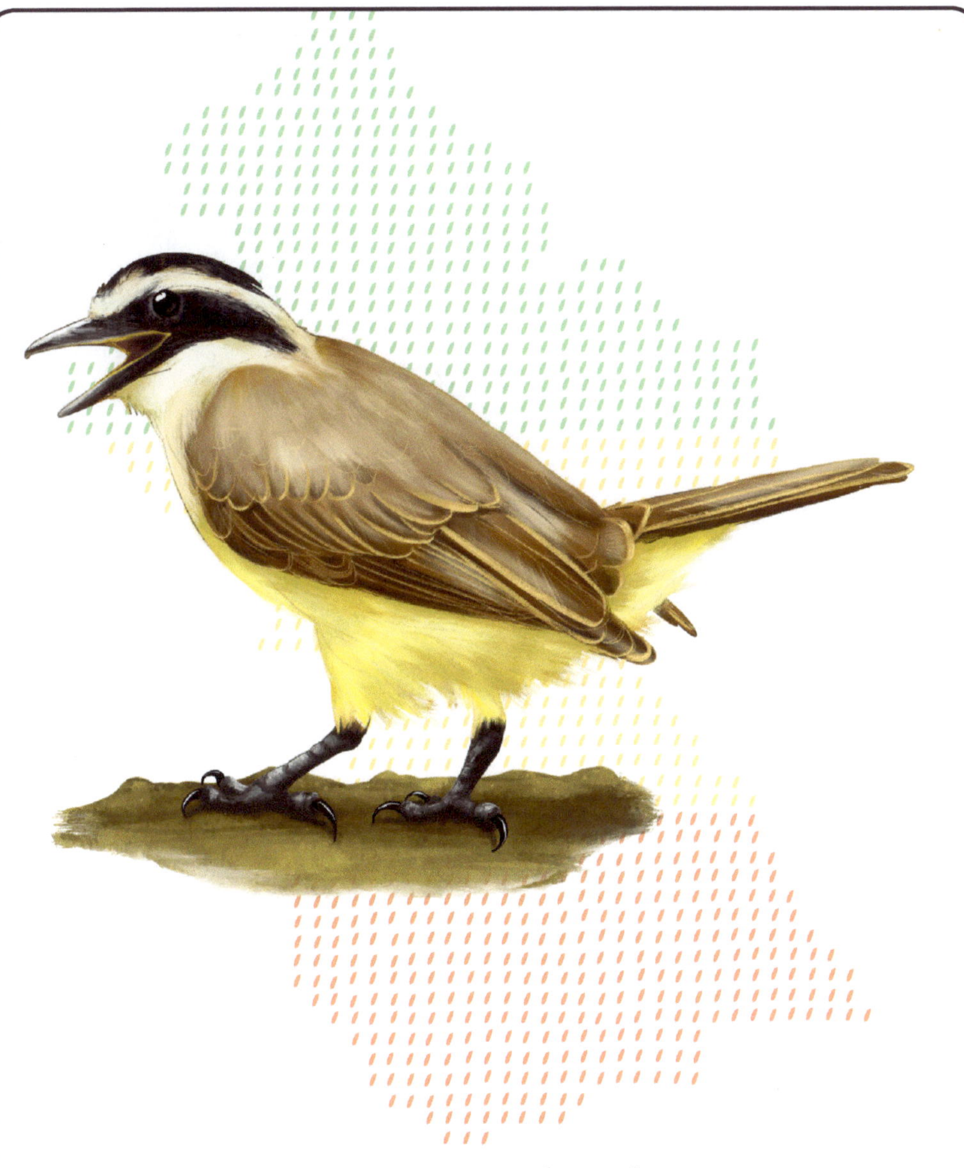

Great Kiskadee

Widespread in the coastal region, it has a distinct call and can be easily recognized, especially in the early morning.

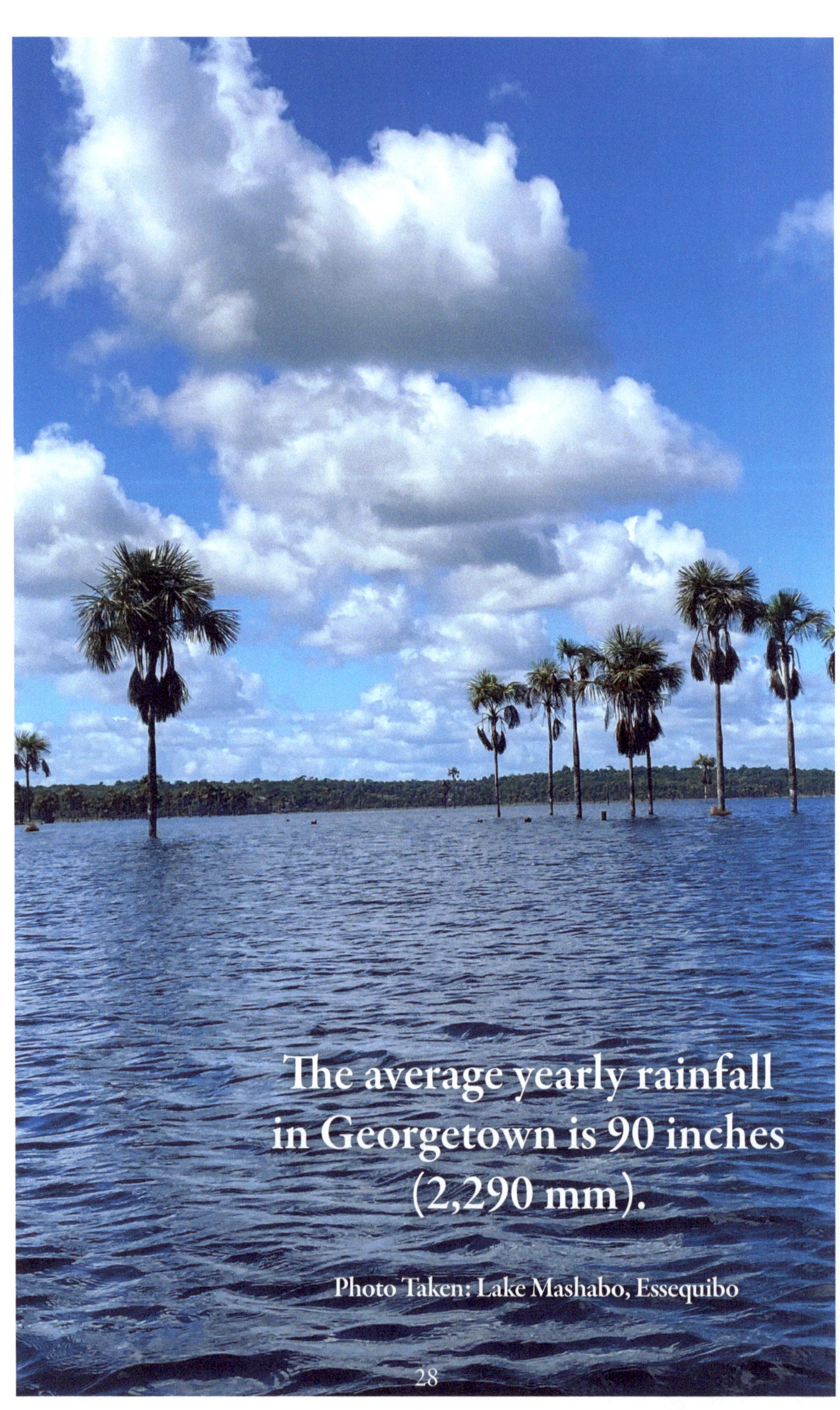

The average yearly rainfall
in Georgetown is 90 inches
(2,290 mm).

Photo Taken: Lake Mashabo, Essequibo

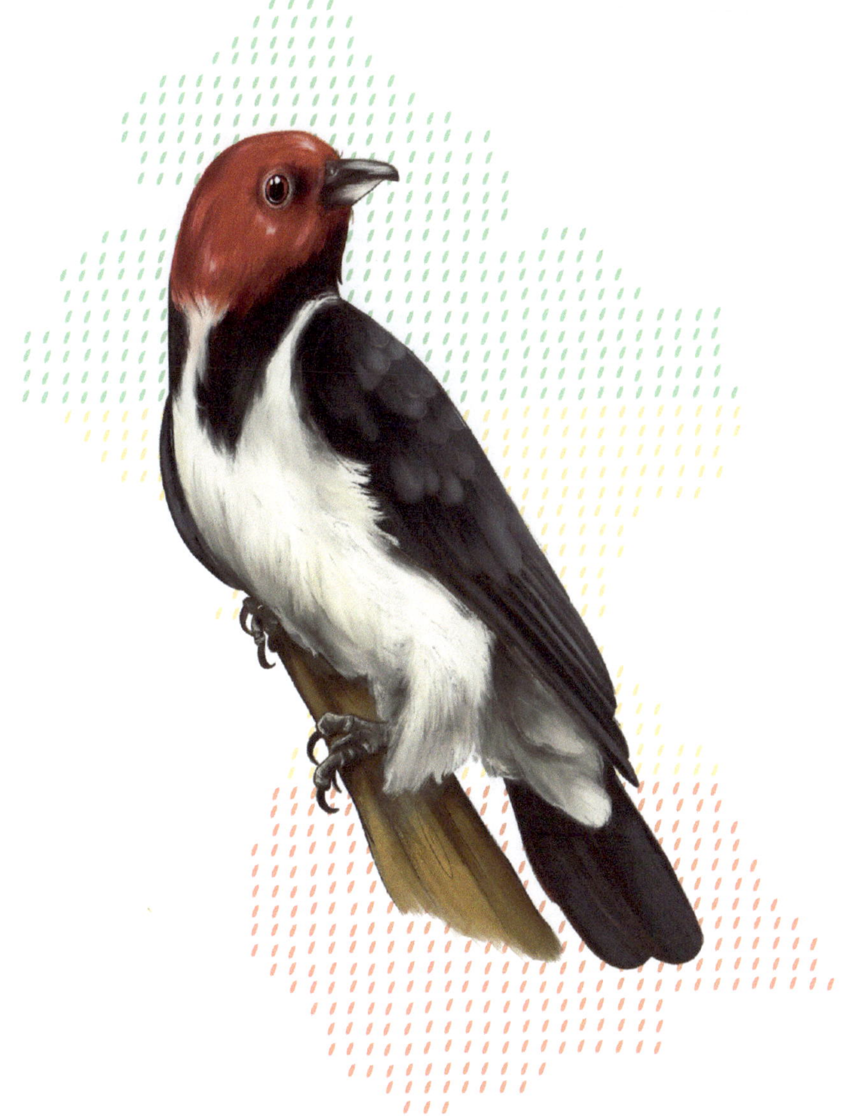

Red-capped Cardinal

Widespread in Guyana's lowland regions, its beautiful red cap makes it stand out in the rice fields.

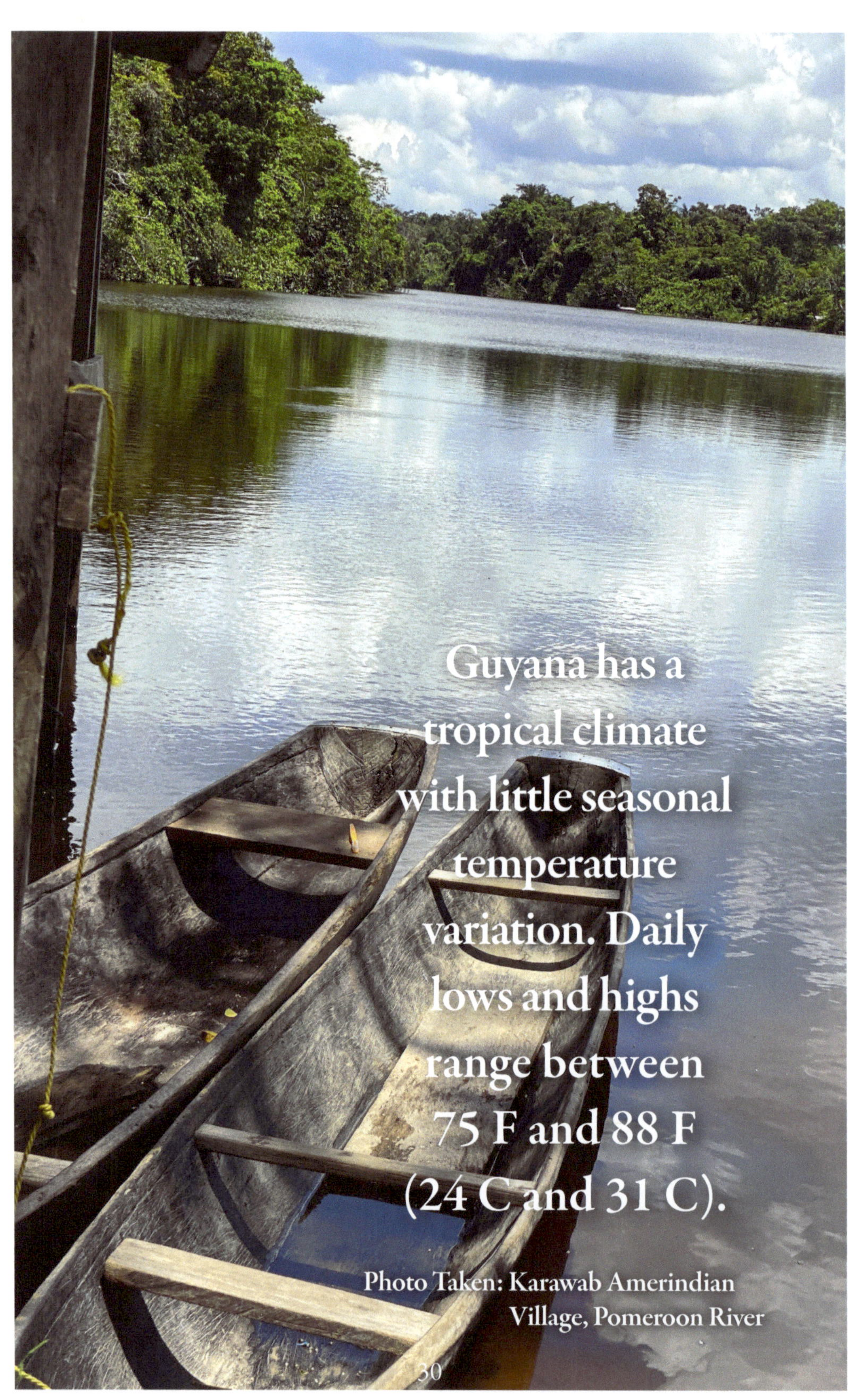

Photo Taken: Karawab Amerindian Village, Pomeroon River

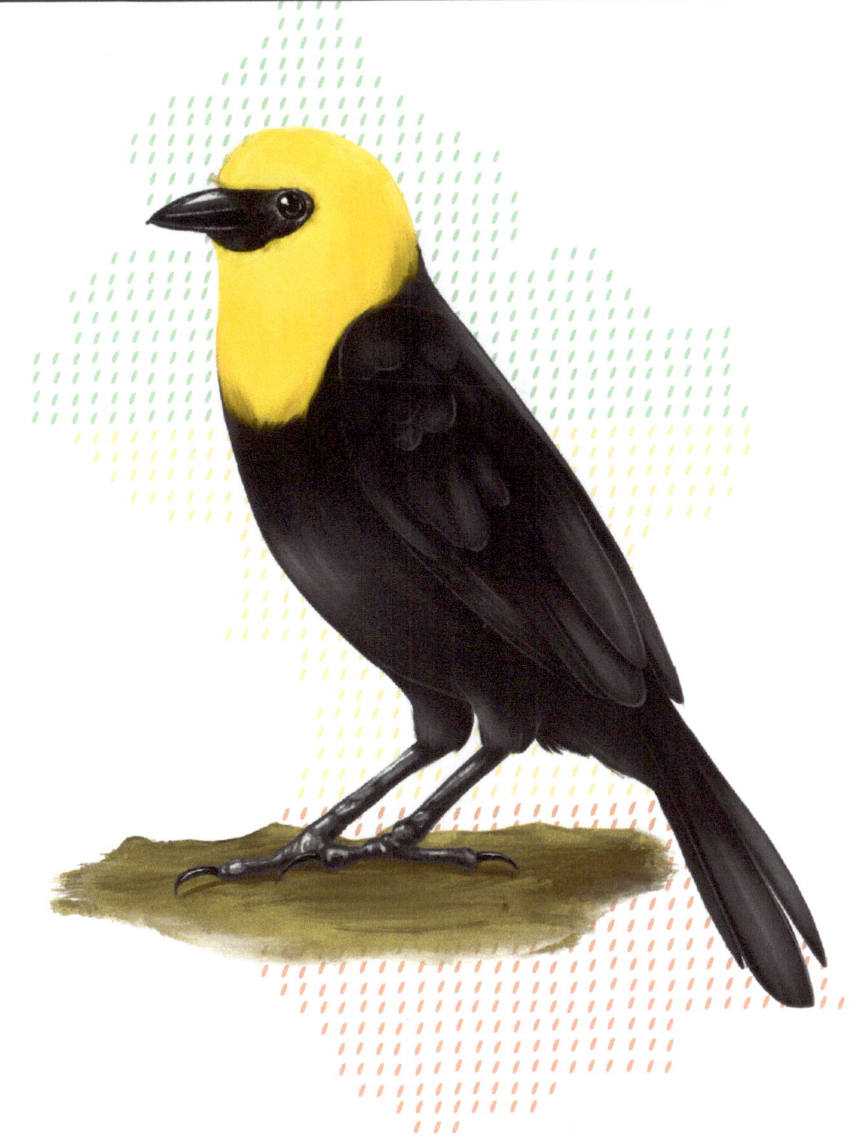

Yellow-hooded Blackbird

Similar to the yellow-headed blackbird of North America, it can be found in the freshwater region of Guyana.

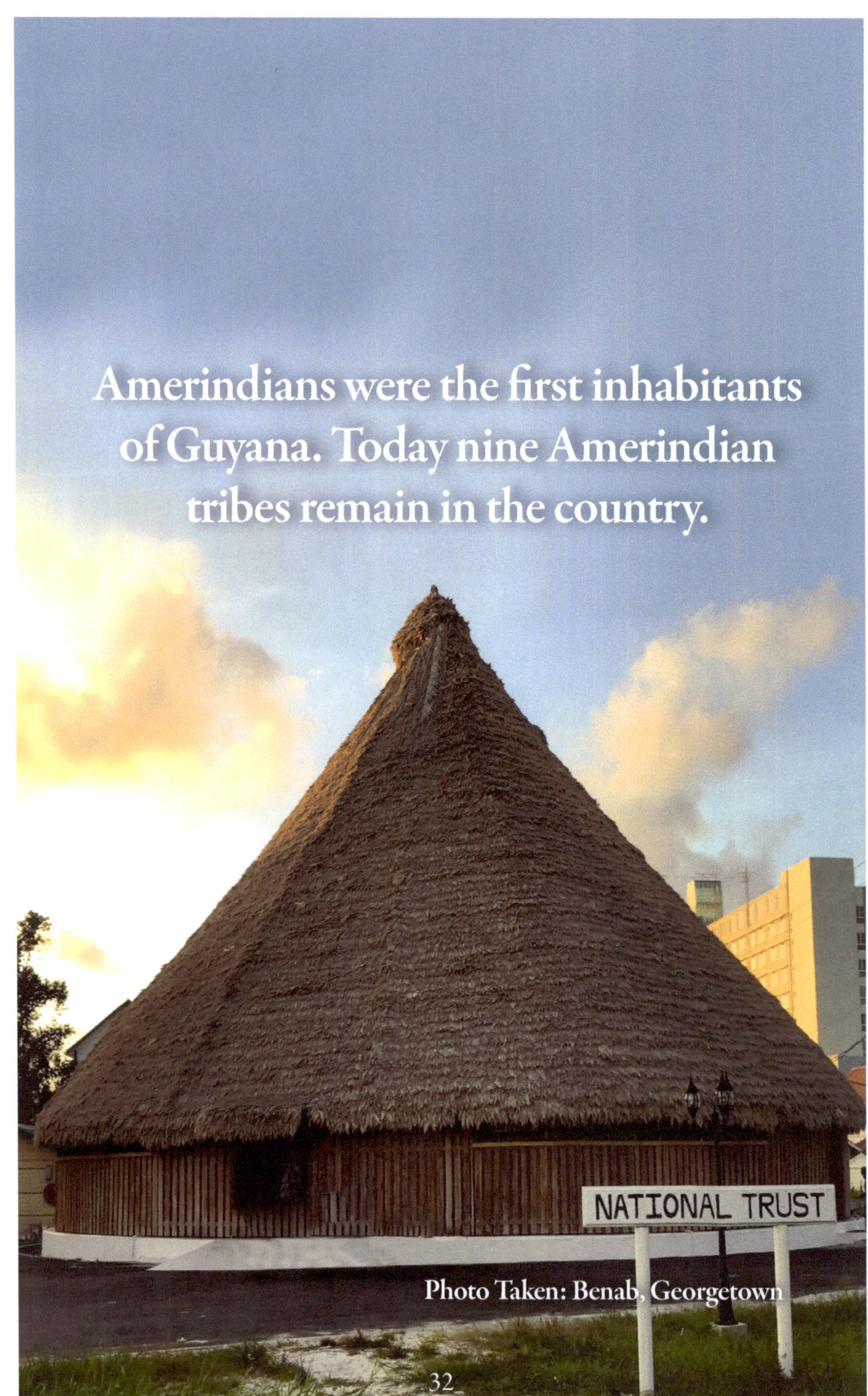

Photo Taken: Benab, Georgetown

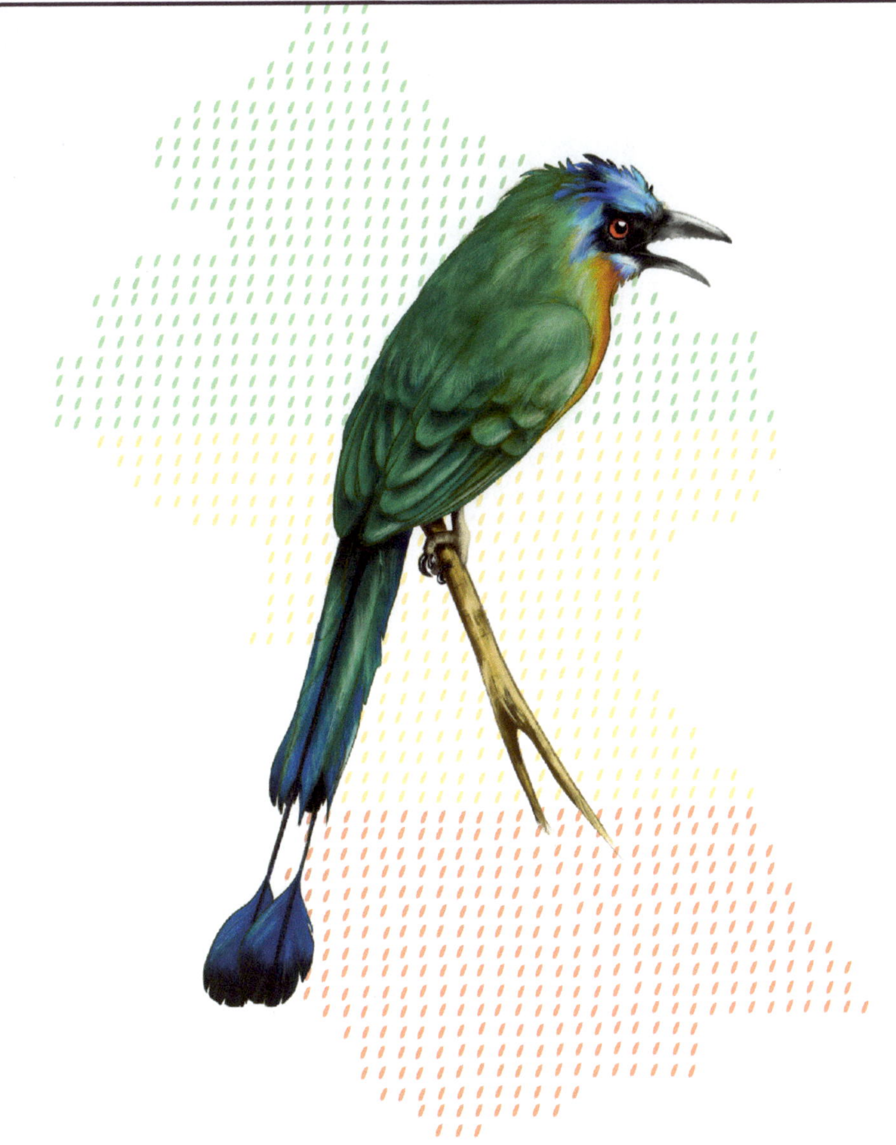

Amazonian Motmot

Found in the rainforests of Guyana, it eats mainly insects, small reptiles, and fruits.

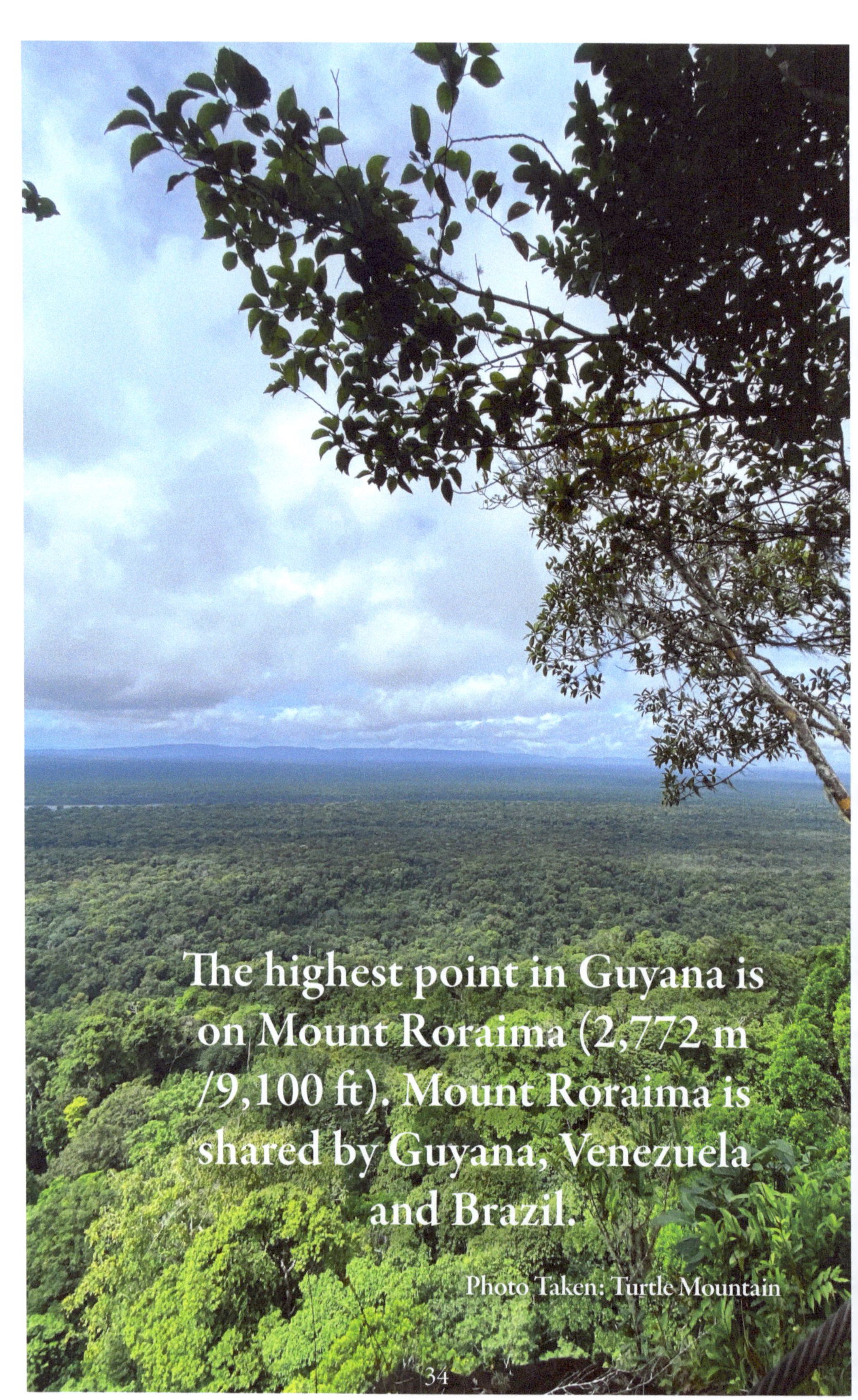

The highest point in Guyana is on Mount Roraima (2,772 m /9,100 ft). Mount Roraima is shared by Guyana, Venezuela and Brazil.

Photo Taken: Turtle Mountain

Notes

Checklist

Hoatzin	
American Pygmy Kingfisher	
Black -collared Hawk	
Black-necked Aracari	
Blue and Yellow Macaw	
Guianan Cock-of-the-Rock	
Orange-winged Parrot	
White Throated Toucan	
Violaceous Euphonia	
Green Tailed Jacamar	
Tourquoise Tanager	
Red-necked Woodpecker	
Harpy Eagle	
Great Kiskadee	
Red-capped Cardinal	
Yellow-hooded Blackbird	
Amazonian Motmot